teach
yourself

word 2002

teach ®
yourself

word 2002

moira stephen

The **teach yourself** series does
exactly what it says, and it
works. For over 60 years, more
than 40 million people have
learnt over 750 subjects the
teach yourself way, with
impressive results.

be where you want to be
with **teach yourself**

For UK orders: please contact Bookpoint Ltd., 130 Milton Park, Abingdon, Oxon OX14 4SB. Telephone: +44 (0)/1235 827720. Fax: +44 (0)/1235 400454. Lines are open 09.00–18.00, Monday to Saturday, with a 24-hour message answering service. You can also order through our website www.madaboutbooks.com.

For USA order enquiries: please contact McGraw-Hill Customer Services, PO Box 545, Blacklick, OH 43004-0545, USA. Telephone: 1-800-722-4726. Fax: 1-614-755-5645.

For Canada order enquiries: please contact McGraw-Hill Ryerson Ltd., 300 Water St, Whitby, Ontario L1N 9B6, Canada. Telephone: 905 430 5000. Fax: 905 430 5020.

Long renowned as the authoritative source for self-guided learning – with more than 30 million copies sold worldwide – the *Teach Yourself* series includes over 300 titles in the fields of languages, crafts, hobbies, business, computing and education.

British Library Cataloguing in Publication Data
A catalogue record for this title is available from The British Library.

Library of Congress Catalog Card Number: On file.

First published in UK 2003 by Hodder Headline Plc., 338 Euston Road, London, NW1 3BH.

First published in US 2003 by Contemporary Books, A Division of The McGraw-Hill Companies, 1 Prudential Plaza, 130 East Randolph Street, Chicago, Illinois 60601 USA.

The 'Teach Yourself' name and logo are registered trade marks of Hodder & Stoughton Ltd.

Typeset by MacDesign, Southampton
Printed in Great Britain for Hodder & Stoughton Educational, a division of Hodder Headline Plc, 338 Euston Road, London NW1 3BH by Cox & Wyman Ltd., Reading, Berkshire.

Impression number   10 9 8 7 6 5 4 3 2 1

Year   2007 2006 2005 2004 2003

contents

01

getting started

In this chapter you will learn

- what you need to run Word 2002
- how to install the software
- how to start Word
- about the Word screen and its tools
- how to use the Help system

Aims of this chapter

This chapter will introduce you to the word processing package Word 2002. We will start with an overview and consider the hardware and software specification required to run Word successfully. We then move on to look at how you install the package on your computer. Getting into Word, the working environment, on-line Help system and exiting Word will also be discussed.

1.1 Introducing Word

Word is a very powerful word processor – but don't let that put you off! It can be used to create simple letters, memos and reports – you'll soon discover how easy it is to generate these documents. You can also use the more sophisticated features in Word to produce mail shots, forms, newsletters and multi-page publications. Word integrates well with other packages in the Microsoft Office suite, which will help you create professional documents that combine files generated in other applications. Finally, if you have Internet access, you'll soon find out how easy it is to use Word with the wider world! You'll learn how to hyperlink to documents and Internet addresses, send e-mails and publish documents on the Web!

It is assumed that you have a working knowledge of Windows.

1.2 Hardware and software requirements

The hardware and software specifications given are for Office XP.

The recommended configuration is a PC with Windows 2000 or XP, a Pentium processor and 128 Mb of RAM.

The minimum specification is as follows:

Personal computer	Pentium 133 MHz or higher processor
Operating system	Windows 98, Windows Me, Windows NT 4.0 with Service Pack 6 or later, Windows 2000, or Windows XP.
RAM	Depends on the operating system used, plus 8MB for each office application in use at one time. **Windows 98**: 24 MB of RAM **Windows Me or NT**: 32 MB of RAM **Windows 2000 or XP**: 64 MB of RAM
Hard disk	Approximately 245 MB of hard disk space in total, with 115 MB on the hard disk where the operating system is installed.
CD-ROM drive	The software is only supplied on CD
Monitor	Super VGA or higher-resolution
Mouse	Microsoft Mouse, IntelliMouse® or compatible pointing device

See **http://www.microsoft.com/uk/office/evaluation/ sysreqs.asp** for full details of system requirements.

1.3 Installing Word

If you have bought a new computer at the same time as your software, the software was most probably pre-installed. If this is the case you can skip this bit and go on to section 1.4.

Word is supplied in all of the Microsoft Office XP editions.

Standard: Word, Excel, Outlook and PowerPoint.

Professional: As Standard plus Access and FrontPage.

Developer: As Professional plus FrontPage, Sharepoint Team Services, Developer tools.

Professional with Publisher: (only available pre-installed).

Small Business: Word, Excel, Outlook and Publisher (only available pre-installed).

These instructions are for installing Microsoft Office:

1 Insert Disk 1 into the CD-ROM drive
2 Follow the instructions on your screen
3 Repeat the process for the other disks

1.4 Starting Word 2002

Starting through the Shortcut Bar:

♦ Click the **Word** tool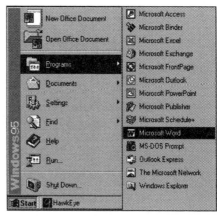

From the Start menu:

1 Click the **Start** button on the Taskbar
2 Point to **Programs**
3 Click **Microsoft
   Word**

1.5 The Word screen

Whichever method you prefer to use to start Word, you are presented with a new blank document, so you can just start typing in your text.

We'll take a tour of the Word screen, so that you know what the various areas are called. You'll find the screen areas referred to by their 'proper' names in the on-line Help, throughout this book and in other publications on the package.

Menus and toolbars

Office XP applications personalize your menus and toolbars automatically. The items that you use most often are featured on your personalized toolbars or menus.

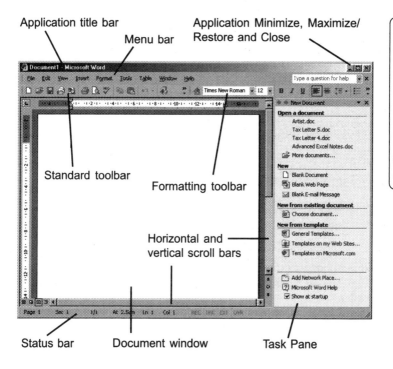

Application title bar

Menu bar

Application Minimize, Maximize/
Restore and Close

Standard toolbar

Formatting toolbar

Horizontal and
vertical scroll bars

Status bar   Document window   Task Pane

Once you start using Word, you'll find that the menu options most recently used will be displayed first when you open a menu (this is your personalized menu). You can expand the menus to reveal all commands (simply click on the down arrow that appears at the bottom of each menu). You may find that the menu automatically expands if you just wait once you've opened it. If you wish to modify the way that the menus work, open the **View** menu choose **Toolbars, Customize.** You can switch the **Always show full menus,** or **Show full menus after a short delay** options on or off on the **Options** tab.

The Standard and Formatting toolbars share a single row, so you have more room for your work (if you wish to disable the row sharing option see section 13.2). When you click a button on a toolbar, that button is added to the personalized toolbar on your screen.

Don't panic if your toolbars and menus are not exactly the same as those illustrated in this book.

Task Pane

When Word is installed on your machine, the Task Pane for creating and opening files is set to display at Startup. This means that the Task Pane appears down the right side of the screen each time that you start Word. You can easily close the Task Pane by clicking the close button at the top right of it.

If you don't want the Task Pane displayed each time that you start Word, deselect the **Show at startup** checkbox at the bottom of the pane. The next time you start Word the Task Pane will not be displayed.

To display the Task Pane:

1 Open the **View** menu

2 Select **Task Pane**

You will encounter a number of Task Panes when working in Word. The **Office Clipboard** Task Pane can be used when copying and moving items (see 2.10) and the Styles and **Formatting**, and **Reveal Formatting** Task Panes are useful when formatting your document (see Chapter 3 and 6). Task Panes are also used when doing Mail Merge (Chapter 10), inserting Clip Art (Chapter 11) and searching for files.

Smart Tags

As you work with Word you will notice that 'smart tags' appear at various times, e.g. when Word automatically corrects the use of capitals, when you paste an item (see 2.10), when using automatic numbering (see 3.10), etc.
If you click the smart tag it will display the options that allow you to control the task that you are performing.

> Now
>
> | | |
> |---|---|
> | ⌨ | Undo Automatic Capitalization |
> | | Stop Auto-capitalizing First Letter of Sentences |
> | | Stop Auto-capitalizing After "be." |
> | ✄ | Control AutoCorrect Options... |

1.6 Menus

There are nine main menus in Word, which you can use to access any function or feature. I suggest you have a browse through them to get an idea of what's available – some menu items may appear familiar to you, some will be new.

You can display menus and select options using the mouse or keyboard.

Using the mouse

1   Click on the menu name to display the list of options available in that menu

2   Click on the menu item you wish to use

◆   Click the extension arrow at the bottom to display all the options available.

Using the keyboard

Each menu name has one character underlined.

To open a menu:

◆   Hold down the [**Alt**] key and press the underlined letter, e.g. [**Alt**]-[**F**] for the **File** menu, [**Alt**]-[**I**] for the **Insert** menu.

Each item in a menu list also has a letter underlined in it.

To select an item from the menu list either:

◆   Press the appropriate letter

Or

◆   Use the up and down arrow keys on your keyboard until the item you want is selected, then press [**Enter**].

Once a menu list is displayed, you can press the right or left arrow keys to move from one menu to another.

To close a menu without selecting an item from the list:

◆   Click the menu name again, click anywhere off the menu list or press [**Esc**] on your keyboard.

In addition to the menus, many commands can be initiated using the toolbars, keyboard shortcuts or shortcut menus. Each of these areas will be covered as you progress through the book.

1.7 Help!

As you work with Word you will most probably find that you come a bit unstuck from time to time and need help! There are several ways of getting help – most of them very intuitive and user friendly.

Office Assistant

To call on the Office Assistant, press [F1] or click the **Help** tool 🔲, or click the

Assistant icon 🔲 on the status bar.

Depending on what you have been doing, the Assistant may display a list of topics that you might be interested in.

* To choose a topic from the **What would you like to do?** list, simply click on the topic.

* If you have a specific question you want to ask, type it in at the prompt and click the **Search** button.

The Assistant will display the Help page.

Some Help pages contain text in a different coloured font – usually blue. If the text is part of a list, click it to expand or collapse the Help item. If the coloured text is embedded within the main text on a page it is probably a phrase or some jargon that has an explanation or definition attached to it. Simply click the coloured text to toggle the display of the definition.

When you've finished exploring the Help system, click the Close button at the top right of the Help window.

The Office Assistant can remain visible as you work on your document, or you can hide it and call on it as required. If you opt to leave it displayed, drag it to an area of your screen where it doesn't obscure your work.

* If you leave the Office Assistant displayed, left-click on it any time you want to ask a question.

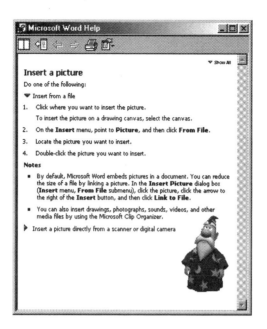

* To hide the Office Assistant, right-click on it and choose **Hide** from the pop-up menu.

To customize the Office Assistant

You can customize the Office Assistant to take on a different appearance, or behave in a different way.

1 Show the Office Assistant (press **[F1]**, click the **Help** tool or click on the Status bar)

2 Click the **Options** button

3 To change its appearance, select the **Gallery** tab and browse through the options available (use the **Next** and **Back** buttons to move through the various guises)

* If you find an Assistant you would like to use, click **OK**.

* To leave the Assistant as it was, click **Cancel**.

4 To change its behaviour, select the **Options** tab, select or deselect the options as required – click on an option to switch it on (ticked) or off

- If you don't want to use the Office Assistant, you can switch it off on the Options tab – simply deselect the *Use the Office Assistant* checkbox.

5   Click **OK** to set the options selected or **Cancel** to leave things as they were

Tips

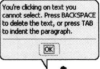

The Office Assistant is constantly monitoring your actions. If it thinks that it has a tip that may be useful to you, a light bulb will light up beside it.

- To read its tip, click the bulb.

Ask a question box

You can also access the Help system using the **Ask a question** box on the Menu bar. Type in your question and press [**Enter**]. Choose the Help topic required from the list that is displayed – click on it.

What's This?

If you haven't used Microsoft Office before, or if you're new to Windows, there may be tools, menus, buttons and areas on your screen that puzzle you. The *What's This?* feature can help.

To find out what a tool does:

1   Hold down the [**Shift**] key and press [**F1**]

2   Click the tool

To find out about an item in a menu list:

1   Hold down the [**Shift**] key and press [**F1**]

2   Open the menu list and select the option from the list

To find out about anything else within the application window:

1   Hold down the [**Shift**] key and press [**F1**]

2   Click on the item

If you accidentally invoke the *What's This* help option, press [**Shift**]-[**F1**] (or the [**Esc**] key) to cancel it.

Contents and Index

Whether or not you opt to use the Office Assistant, the Help 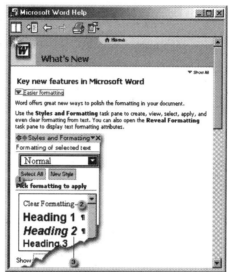 button will open the on-line Help system. You can also access it from the Help menu.

Once you have opened the Help system you can interrogate it using the Contents, Answer Wizard or Index tabs.

Click the button to toggle the display of the tabs.

Contents tab

You can browse through the Help from the Contents tab.

* Click + beside a book to display or – to hide its contents list.

When a book is open, you will be presented with a list of topics

To display a topic:

1 Click on it

2 Work through the Help system to find the Help you need

To print a topic:

* Click the **Print** button 🖨 in the **Help** dialog box when the topic is displayed.

To revisit pages you've already been to:

* Click the **Back** ⇦ or **Forward** ⇨ buttons to move through the pages.

Close the Help window when you're finished.

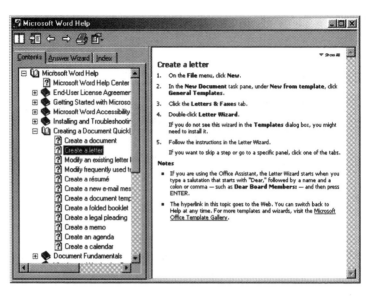

Answer Wizard

If you want to interrogate the Help system, try the Answer Wizard tab.

1 Enter your question, e.g. *How do I insert a picture* and click Search

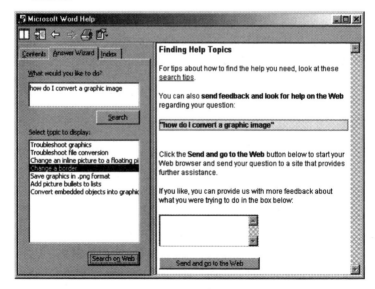

2 Select a topic from the *Select topic to display* list

• The Help page will be displayed

If the topics listed don't provide the information that you need, click on the **Search on Web** button and send your question to the Web Help system.

Index tab

If you know what you are looking for, the Index tab gives you quick access to any topic and is particularly useful once you are familiar with the terminology used in Word.

1 At the **Microsoft Word Help** dialog box, select the **Index** tab

2 Type the word in the *Type Keywords* field and click **Search**

Or

• Double-click on a word in the *Or choose keywords* list

3 Choose a topic from the *Choose a topic* list

4 Work through the Help system until you find what you are looking for

5 Close the Help window when you've finished

ScreenTips

If you point to any tool on a displayed toolbar, a ScreenTip will probably appear to describe the purpose of the tool.

If no ScreenTips appear, you can easily switch them on if you want to.

If you like using keyboard shortcuts, you may find it useful to customize the basic ScreenTip, so that it displays the keyboard shortcut for a command as well. This might help you learn the keyboard shortcuts more quickly.

To switch ScreenTips on or off, or to display keyboard shortcuts:

1 Point to any toolbar and click the right mouse button

2 Choose **Customize...** from the shortcut menu

3 In the Customize dialog box select the **Options** tab

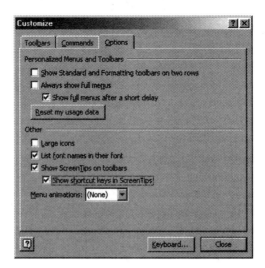

4 To switch the ScreenTips on, select the *Show ScreenTips on toolbars* option (if you don't like ScreenTips, untick this to switch them off)

5 Select the *Show shortcut keys in ScreenTips* option to have the keyboard shortcut for each tool displayed in the ScreenTip

6 Click **Close**

Dialog Box Help

When you access a dialog box in Word e.g. the Customize one above, you can get Help on any item within it that you don't understand. To get Help on an item in a dialog box:

1 Click the ▣ button at the right of the dialog box title bar

2 Click on an option, button or item in the dialog box that you want explained

• A brief explanation of the item will be displayed.

3 Click anywhere within the dialog box to cancel the explanation

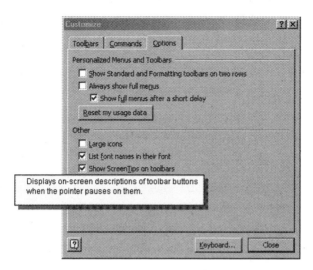

1.8 Help on the Internet

If you can't find the help you are looking for in the normal Help system, visit the Microsoft Office Update Web site to get updated Help files, answers to frequently-asked questions, tips, templates and articles about Word.

1 Open the **Help** menu

2 Choose **Office on the Web**

3 Navigate your way through the Help pages until you find the information required

1.9 Exiting Word

When you have finished working in Word you must close the application down – don't just switch off your computer!

To exit Word

♦ Open the **File** menu and choose **Exit**.

Or

♦ Click the **Close** button ☒ in the right-hand corner of the Application Title Bar.

If you have been working on a document, but have not saved it, you will be prompted to do so – see *Save and Save As* in section 2.4.

Summary

In this chapter we have discussed:

*   The fact that Word is a very powerful, yet easy to use, word processing package.

*   The minimum software and hardware requirements necessary to run the package successfully.

*   The installation procedure for the software.

*   Accessing the package through the Start menu and the Shortcut Bar.

*   The Word screen.

*   Operating the menu system, using the mouse and the keyboard.

*   The Office Assistant and On-line Help system.

*   Help from the Microsoft Office Update Web site.

*   Exiting Word.

02

basic word skills

In this chapter you will learn

- how to create, save, print, open and close documents
- about proofing documents
- some basic editing techniques
- how to move and copy text
- about viewing options

Aims of this chapter

In this chapter we will discuss the basic word processing skills you will need to acquire. By the time you have completed this chapter, you will know how to create, save, print, open and close documents. Spelling and grammar checking together with simple editing techniques for inserting, deleting, copying and moving text are covered, as are some options for viewing your document on screen.

2.1 Your first document

When you start Word, a new document is created automatically – all that you need to do is type in your text. The document name, *Document1*, is displayed on the document title bar. Each new document you create during a session in Word is given a name following the *Document1* format. Your second document will be called *Document2*, and so on. These names should be considered temporary – when you save your document, give it a new, meaningful name.

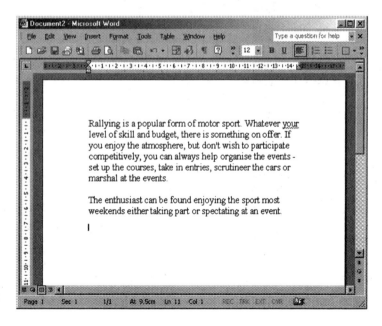

If the Task Pane is displayed, close it (see 1.5).

The insertion point – the flashing black vertical bar – is in the top left of the text area on the first page. Just type. Your text will appear at the insertion point.

Things to remember when entering text into your document:

- DO NOT press [**Enter**] at the end of each line of text. If a sentence is going to run onto a new line, let it – the text will be wrapped automatically at the end of the line.

- DO press [**Enter**] at the end of short lines of text, e.g. after lines in an address at the top of a letter or after the last line in a paragraph.

- To leave a clear line between paragraphs, or several empty lines between headings or in the signature block at the end of a letter, press [**Enter**] as often as is necessary to get the effect you want.

2.2 Spelling and grammar

To help you produce accurate work, Word can check the spelling and grammar in your document. You can either:

- Let Word check your spelling and grammar as you work, and draw attention to any errors as you make them.

Or

- Check the spelling and grammar in your document when you are ready, and correct any errors at that stage.

Checking spelling and grammar as you work

This option is operational by default – if it doesn't work on your system, someone has switched it off.

- As you enter your text, any words that Word thinks are incorrectly spelt will be underlined with a red, wavy line.

- Any words, phrases or sentences that have unusual capitalization or aren't grammatically correct will have a grey wavy line.

To find out what Word thinks you should have done in place of what you actually did, right-click (click the right mouse button) on the highlighted word or phrase and respond to the suggestions as appropriate.

The error has a wavy underline

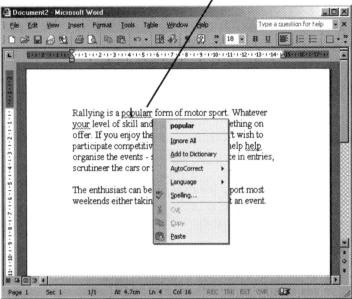

In the example above, 'popular' has been spelt incorrectly – when you right-click on it any possible correct spellings (found in Word's dictionary) are listed at the top of the shortcut menu.

- If you wish to change the word to one of those listed, click on the word that you want to use in the shortcut menu.

- If the word that is underlined is correctly spelt, it's just that Word doesn't recognize the word because it isn't in its dictionary. You can choose to **Ignore All** or **Add to Dictionary**.

- If you choose **Ignore All**, Word will not highlight the word again in this document in this working session (it will however draw your attention to the word if it appears in another document or in another working session).

- If you choose **Add to Dictionary**, the word will be added to Word's dictionary, and it will be recognized as a correctly spelt word from then on.

Grammatical errors can be dealt with in a similar way. When you right-click on the error, Word will display the problem, and suggest a remedy if it can. You can choose whether you wish to change your text to that suggested or ignore any suggestion made.

Spell and grammar checker options

The automatic spelling and grammar checks can be switched on or off to suit yourself.

1 Open the **Tools** menu and choose **Options**

2 In the **Options** dialog box, select the **Spelling & Grammar** tab

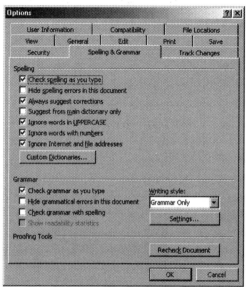

3 Select or deselect the *Check spelling as you type* and *Check grammar as you type* options as required

Other spelling and grammar checking options are displayed in this dialog box. Come back to the Options dialog box and explore it using the on-line Help if your spelling and grammar checkers are not acting as you would expect.

Checking spelling and grammar when you are ready

You can easily check your spelling and grammar at any time using the Spelling and Grammar tool on the Standard toolbar.

To start checking:

1 Click the **Spelling and Grammar** tool ![icon] . Word will check from the insertion point through to the end of your document. Respond to the prompts as you see fit. When the

checking is complete, a prompt will appear to tell you so.

2 Click **OK** to return to your document

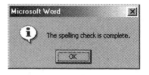

2.3 Simple editing techniques

The spelling and grammar checker will help you locate and fix some of your errors. It will not, however, correct everything.

You may decide to add some more text into the body of your document, or delete some that you no longer wish to use. You can add or delete as much text as you wish!

You can easily insert any characters that you have missed out, or delete any characters that you don't need.

Before you can insert or delete characters within existing text however, you must move the insertion point (the flashing vertical black bar) to the place where you want to edit.

Moving the insertion point

If the text you want to look at is not displayed on your screen, use the scroll bars to bring it into view.

There are many different ways to reposition the insertion point within your text – use the method which suits you.

Using the mouse

1 Position the I-beam (the mouse pointer when over a text area) at the place you want to move the insertion point to

2 Click the left mouse button

To move a character or line at a time:

♦ Press the right, left, up or down arrow (cursor) keys until the insertion point is where you want it.

To move right or left a word at a time:

♦ Hold down [**Ctrl**] and press the right or left arrow key.

To move up or down a paragraph at a time:

♦ Hold down [**Ctrl**] and press the up or down arrow key.

Other useful ones – to move:

- to the end of the line that the insertion point is on – press [**End**].
- to the beginning of the line that the insertion point is in – press [**Home**].
- to the beginning of the document – press [**Ctrl**]-[**Home**].
- to the end of the document – press [**Ctrl**]-[**End**].

Experiment with the various options as you work.

Inserting text

1 Position the insertion point where you want to add text

2 Type in the new text

Deleting text

1 Position the insertion point next to the character that you want to delete

- If the insertion point is to the *right* of the character, press the backspace key [←] once for each character.
- If the insertion point is to the *left*, press the [**Delete**] key once for each character.

Both the [←] and [**Delete**] keys repeat – if you hold them down they will zoom through your text removing it much quicker than you could type it in, so be careful with them!

Overtype

You can type over existing text, replacing the old text with the new in one operation, instead of deleting the old then entering the new.

- To go into Overtype mode, double-click the OVR button on the Status bar. When Overtype mode is on, the text on the button is black.

Position the insertion point within some text and type – watch to see what happens – the existing text will be replaced by the new text.

- To switch Overtype mode off, double-click the OVR button again – the text on the button is dimmed.
- You can also switch the Overtype on and off using [**Insert**] on your keyboard.

2.4 Save and Save As

If you want to keep your file, you must save it. If you don't save your file it will be lost when you exit Word, if the computer crashes, or if there is a power failure. You can save your file at any time – you don't have to wait until you've entered all your text and corrected all the errors. Try to get into the habit of saving your document regularly.

To save your document:

1 Click the **Save** tool 💾 on the Standard toolbar. The **Save As** dialog box will appear on your screen

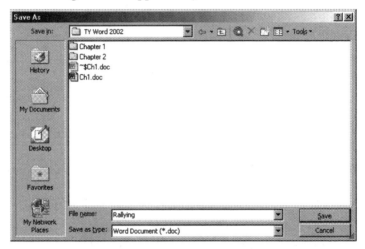

2 Specify the folder into which your file should be saved (the default is *My Documents*)

3 Give your file a name

4 Leave the **Save as type:** field at Word Document

5 Click **Save**

The new file name will appear on the document Title Bar in place of the temporary file name.

As your document develops, you can re-save your file any time you wish – just click the Save tool again. The Save As dialog box will not reappear, but the old version of the file on your disk will be replaced by the new, up-to-date version displayed on your screen.

Save As

There may be times that you save a file, edit it, then decide that you want to save the edited file but also keep the original version of the file on disk.

If you don't want to overwrite the old file with the new version, save it using a different file name. You can save your file to the same folder, or you can select a different drive and/or folder.

1 Open the **File** menu and choose **Save As**
2 The **Save As** dialog box will appear again
3 Enter a new name in the **File name** field
4 Click **Save**

♦ If you save the new version of the file into the same folder as the old one, you must use a different file name.

2.5 Print Preview and Print

At some stage you will want to print your file. Before sending a document to print, it's a good idea to *preview* the document.

Print Preview

The preview will display a full page of your document on the screen at once (more than one page if you wish) so that you can check how the finished page will look.

♦ How much space does your text take up?

♦ Is the balance of 'white space' (blank areas) and text okay?

If the preview looks good, you can send your document to the printer. If not, you might want to edit the layout to try to get a better-looking document.

♦ To preview a document, click the **Print Preview** tool

A full-page preview of your document will appear on screen.

Zoom

If you move the pointer over a page in Print Preview, it looks like a magnifying glass with a + (plus sign) on it.

♦ Click the left mouse button and you will be *zoomed* in on your document so that you can read it.

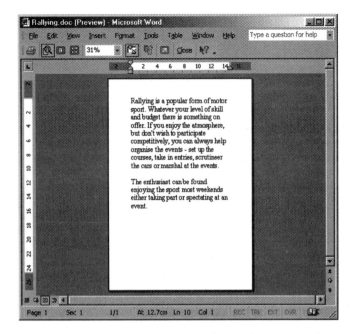

When you are zoomed in, the magnifying glass pointer has a – (minus sign) on it.

- Click to zoom out to get an overview of the page again.

Editing text in Print Preview

If you zoom in on your text, and notice something you want to change, you can edit your document when you are in Print Preview.

- Click the **Magnifier** tool 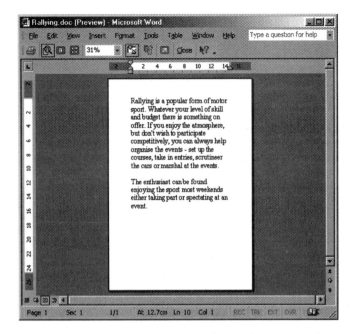 on the Print Preview toolbar.

The insertion point will appear in your document. You can use any editing techniques you wish on the text.

- To enable the zoom feature again, click the **Magnifier** tool.

Print

If you are happy with the appearance of your document, and want to print it out from the preview window, click the **Print** tool 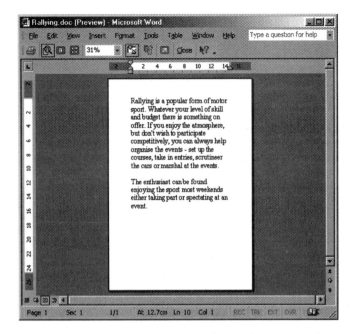 on the toolbar. One copy of your document will be sent to the printer.

Print Preview toolbar

The Print Preview window has its own toolbar which can be used to control the display of your document on the screen. Experiment with the tools to see what effect they have.

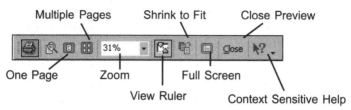

Multiple Pages   Shrink to Fit   Close Preview

One Page   Zoom   Full Screen

View Ruler   Context Sensitive Help

One Page

Click to display one page of your document at a time.

Multiple Pages

This tool drops down a grid that you can click and drag over to indicate the number of pages you want to display at once.

Zoom

This sets the percentage of magnification on your document.

View Ruler

Toggles the display of the vertical and horizontal rulers.

Shrink to Fit

If a small amount of text appears on the last page of your document you may be able to reduce the number of pages by clicking this tool. Word decreases the size of each font used in the document to get the text to fit on to one page less. This works best with relatively short documents – letters, memos, etc.

Full Screen

You can remove most of the toolbars, menu bar, title bar, etc. to get a 'clean screen' display. To return the screen to normal, click **Close Full Screen** on the Full Screen toolbar or press [**Esc**].

Close Preview

Exits Print Preview and returns you to your document.

Context Sensitive Help

Click this tool, then click on a tool, scroll bar, ruler, etc. to get a brief description of its function. Once you've read the information, click anywhere on your screen to close the information box.

Moving through your document in Print Preview

If you have more than one page in your document, you may want to scroll through the pages in Print Preview to check that they look okay. You can do this in a number of ways:

- Click the arrow up or arrow down at the top or bottom of the vertical scroll bar.

- Press the [**PageUp**] or [**PageDown**] keys.

- Click the **Previous Page** or **Next Page** button at the bottom of the vertical scroll bar.

- Drag the scroll box up or down the vertical scroll bar until you reach the page you want to view (notice the prompt that tells you which page you've reached).

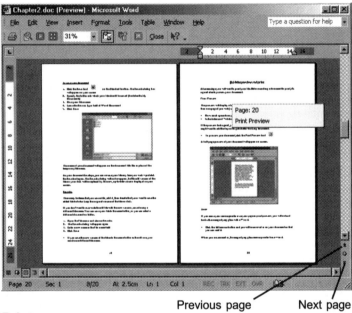

Previous page   Next page

Print

To print one copy of the whole document:

- Click the **Print** tool 🖨 on either the Standard toolbar or the Print Preview toolbar.

If you don't want to print the whole document, you can specify the pages you want printed in the Print dialog box.

1   Open the **File** menu and choose **Print** (or press **[Ctrl]-[P]**)

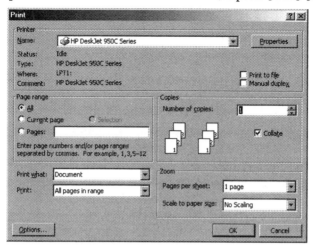

2   At the dialog box, specify the pages you want to print – **All**, **Current page** (the one the insertion point is in) or **Pages**

♦   To print consecutive pages, enter the range in the **Pages** field in the format 5–12 (if you want to print all the pages from 5 through to 12).

♦   To print non-consecutive pages, enter the page numbers separated by commas, in the format 5,7,12,30.

♦   To enter a mixture of consecutive and non-consecutive pages the format is 4,5,6–12,14.

3   Click **OK** once you've specified your page range

2.6 Close

Once you've finished working on a document you should close it. You can have several documents open at the same time when working in Word and sometimes this is very useful. However, depending on how much memory your computer has, you may find that it slows down when you have several documents open. So, if you don't need to have a document open, close it.

To close your document:

♦   Open the **File** menu and choose **Close**.

Or

- Click **Close** ☒ at the top right of the document title bar.

You will be prompted to save the document if it has changed since the last time you saved it.

Shortcut menu

As an alternative to using the toolbars or the menu bar to initiate commands, you may like to try the shortcut menu. If necessary, open a document to try this – see section 2.9.

To display the shortcut menu click the right mouse button. The list of options varies depending on where the insertion point is, or, on what you have selected.

2.7 Create a new blank document

It is very easy to create a new document when working in Word. The instructions here will create a new document using the *blank document template*. A template is simply a pattern on which your document is based – every document you create in Word must take its pattern from a template.

The blank document template has an A4 size page, portrait orientation (tall ways up), with an inch (2.54cm) margin (blank space between the edge of the paper and the text area) at the top and bottom of the page, and an inch and a quarter (3.17cm) margin at the left and right-hand sides.

When you access Word, and are presented with the *Document1* temporary file; that file is based on the blank document template.

To create a new document from the blank document template:

- Click the **New Blank Document** tool ☐ on the Standard toolbar.

A new document will appear on your screen, with the filename *Document2* (the number in the file name depends on how many documents you have created in this working session).

- If the Task Pane is open, you can click **New Blank Document**.

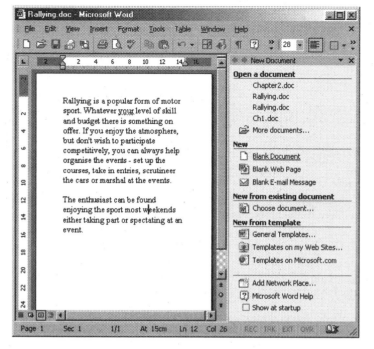

2.8 Opening an existing document

If you want to view, update or print a document that you have already created, saved and closed you must first open it.

To open an existing document:

1   Click the **Open** tool 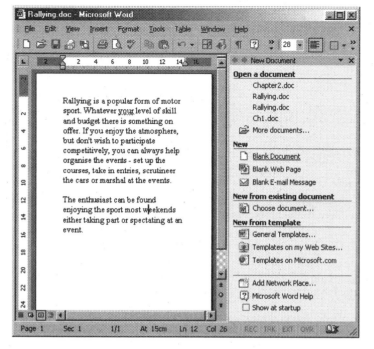 on the Standard toolbar

+   The **Open** dialog box will appear on your screen.

2   Locate the folder that your document is stored in (if necessary)

3   Select the document you wish to open – click on its name

4   Click **Open**

You can also open a document by double-clicking on its name in the Open dialog box.

If the document you want to open is a recently-used file (one of the last four you were working on) you will find its name displayed at the bottom of the File menu and in the Task Pane.

You can open your document from either place, rather than go through the Open dialog box.

1 Open the **File** menu and click on the file name.

Or

♦ Click on the file name in the Task Pane.

If you have more than one document open, you will see their file names displayed on the Taskbar at the bottom of your screen. If you point to the file name on the Taskbar, the full file name and the name of the application will be displayed. To move from one document to another, click on the document name that you want to display.

2.9 Selection techniques

Selection techniques are *very* important in Word. You need to use them if you want to:

♦ Copy or move text within a document.

♦ Copy or move text from one document to another.

♦ Change the formatting of existing text.

♦ Quickly delete large chunks of text.

There are several ways to select text in Word – try some out and use whatever seems easiest for you.

Using the mouse

Click and drag

1 Move the mouse pointer to one end of the block of text

2 Click and hold down the left mouse button

3 Holding the mouse button down, drag over the text until you reach the other end of the text you want to select

4 Release the mouse button

This method tends to work very well for smaller chunks to text – where all the text you want to select is visible on the screen.

If you need to select a big chunk of text, click and drag can be difficult to control – once your text starts to scroll, things move very quickly and it can be hard to see what is being selected.

Click – [Shift] – Click

This method is often easier to control than click and drag.

1 Click at one end of the text you want to select (this positions the insertion point)

2 Move the mouse pointer (do not hold down the mouse button) to the other end of the text

3 Hold down [**Shift**] and click the left mouse button

All the text between the insertion point and the mouse pointer should be selected. If it isn't, you most probably released the [**Shift**] key *before* you clicked – try again if this is the case!

Both the *click and drag* and the *Click – [Shift] – Click* methods can be used to select any amount of text.

If you are selecting a standard unit of text – a word, a sentence, a paragraph or the whole document – there are some special selection techniques that you might like to try instead of those described above.

To select:

◆ A *word* – double-click on it.

◆ A *sentence* – hold down the [**Ctrl**] key and click anywhere within the sentence.

◆ A *paragraph* – double-click in the selection bar to the left of the paragraph you wish to select *or* triple-click anywhere within the paragraph.

◆ *The whole document* – triple-click in the selection bar.

To deselect any unit of text:

◆ Click anywhere within your text, or press one of the arrow keys on your keyboard.

Using the keyboard

If you prefer working with the keyboard rather than the mouse, there are several selection techniques you can try. Selecting text using the keyboard is really a variation on moving through your document using the keyboard (discussed in section 2.3 above).

Try these selection methods. All work from the insertion point.

To select a character or line at a time:

- Hold [**Shift**] down and press the right, left, up or down arrow (cursor) keys until you have selected the text required.

To select right or left, a word at a time:

- Hold down [**Shift**], hold down [**Ctrl**] and press the right or left arrow key until you have selected the text you need.

To select up or down a paragraph at a time:

- Hold down [**Shift**], hold down [**Ctrl**] and press the up or down arrow key until you have selected the required text.

Other useful ones are:

- [**Shift**]-[**End**] to select to the end of the line.
- [**Shift**]-[**Home**] to select to the beginning of the line.
- [**Shift**]-[**Ctrl**]-[**Home**] to select to the beginning of the document.
- [**Shift**]-[**Ctrl**]-[**End**] to select to the end of the document.
- [**Ctrl**]-[**A**] to select the whole document.

Experiment with the various options as you work.

2.10 Cut, Copy and Paste

When working on a document, you will sometimes find that you have entered the correct text but it's in the wrong place! It may be that it should be somewhere else in that document, or you might want it to go into another document. You could delete the text and type it in again at the correct place, but it's much quicker (especially if it's more than a couple of words) to move or copy the text to its new location.

- You can *move* the text from its current position and place it elsewhere in the same or another document.
- If you want to keep the text, but repeat it in another place in the same or another document, you can copy it.

You can move or copy any amount of text – a word, several sentences or paragraphs, or a whole document – but first you must select it (see section 2.9).

Moving text (Cut and Paste)

1 Select the text you want to move

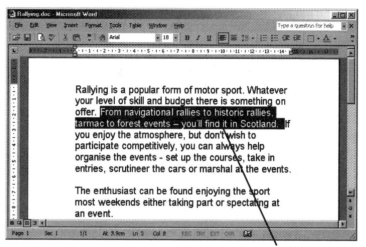

Selected sentence

2 Click the **Cut** tool ✂ on the Standard toolbar

3 Position the insertion point where you want the text to go

4 Click the **Paste** tool 📋 on the Standard toolbar

The text will appear at the insertion point.

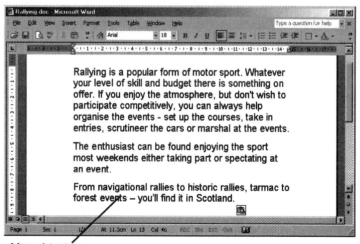

Moved text

◆ To specify the format of the pasted item, click the Paste options smart tag (it appears below the item) and select the option required.

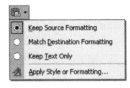

Copying text (Copy and Paste)

Copying text uses a similar technique, but the copied text remains in place, and a copy of it appears at the insertion point.

1 Select the text you want to copy

2 Click the **Copy** tool on the Standard toolbar

3 Position the insertion point where you want the text to go

4 Click the **Paste** tool on the Standard toolbar

A copy of the original text will appear at the insertion point.

Office Clipboard

If you cut or copy a couple of items, the Office Clipboard task pane will appear automatically. You can also display this task pane by choosing **Office Clipboard** from the **Edit** menu. The Task Pane shows a list of the items that you have cut or copied. You can store up to 24 items in the Office Clipboard.

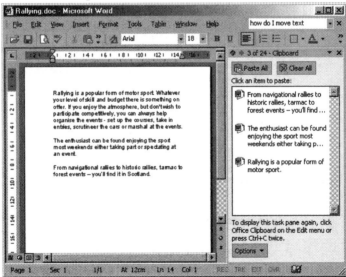

- To paste an individual item from the Clipboard, click on it in the Task Pane.

- To paste all the items, click **Paste All** at the top of the pane.

- To empty the Clipboard, click **Clear All** at the top of the pane.

- To specify how you want the Office Clipboard Task Pane to work, click the **Options** at the bottom of the pane and select or deselect the options as required.

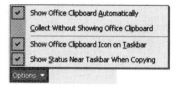

A clipboard icon appears on the Taskbar when the Task Pane is displayed.

- Click the **Close** button at the top right of the Task Pane when you have finished using it.

Cut or Copy to a different document

You can move or copy text from one document to another. It's usually easier if you first open the document you want to move or copy the text from and also the document you want to paste into. You can have several documents open at the same time when working in Word.

To go from one open document to another use the Taskbar or the **Window** menu – you will find a list of your open documents at the end of it. The document currently displayed on screen is the one that has a tick beside its name in the Window menu.

To display another open document, open the **Window** menu and click on the name of the document you want to look at.

To move or copy text from one document to another:

1 Open the document you want to move or copy text from (the source document)

2 Open the document you want to move or copy the text to (the destination document)

3 Display the document you want to move or copy text from

4 Select the text you want to move or copy

5 Click the **Cut** or **Copy** tool on the Standard toolbar

6 Display the document you want to move or copy the text to

7 Position the insertion point where you want the text to go

8 Click the **Paste** tool on the Standard toolbar

Your text will appear at the insertion point.

2.11   Drag and drop

As an alternative to using Cut or Copy and Paste techniques to move and copy text, you may find *drag and drop* useful.

Drag and drop is especially useful when moving or copying a small amount of text a short distance – i.e. to somewhere else on the screen. If you try to drag and drop text a long way, you will probably find that the text scrolls very quickly on the screen and is very hard to control.

To move:

1 Select the text that you want to move

2 Position the mouse pointer anywhere over the selected text

3 Click and hold down the left button (notice the 'ghost' insertion point that appears within the selected text area)

4 Drag your mouse until the ghost insertion point is where you want your text moved to

5 Release the mouse button

To copy:

Copying text is just like moving it, but this time you hold down [**Ctrl**].

1 Select the text that you want to copy

2 Position the mouse pointer anywhere over the selected text

3 Hold down [**Ctrl**]

4 Click and hold down the left mouse button

5 Drag your mouse until the ghost insertion point is where you want your text moved to

6 Release the mouse button

7 Release [**Ctrl**]

2.12 Undo

If you make a mistake when you are working, don't panic! You may be able to *undo* what you just did by clicking the **Undo** tool [icon] on the Standard toolbar.

If the action you want to undo was not the last thing you did, click the drop-down arrow to the right of the tool to display a list of the actions that you can undo. Scroll through the list if necessary until you find the action you want to undo and click on it. When you undo an action from the list, all the actions above the one you click will also be undone.

If you change your mind, click the **Redo** tool [icon] to put things back as they were, or click the drop-down arrow to the right of the tool and select the action you want to redo from the list.

If the Redo tool is dimmed, you have not *undone* anything that can be redone!

2.13 Normal vs Print Layout view

When working in a document, there are several viewing options available. The viewing option you select controls how your document looks on the screen – not how it will print out.

You will usually work in Normal view when entering your text, but Print Layout view is useful if you want to see where your text actually appears on the page.

Normal view

Normal view is the pre-set view for working in Word. It is the view usually used for entering, editing and formatting text.

The page layout is simplified in Normal View. Margins, headers and footers, multiple columns, pictures, etc. are not displayed.

To change to Normal view:

1 Open the **View** menu
2 Choose **Normal**

Or

♦ Click the **Normal View** tool ▦ at the bottom left of the screen.

Print Layout view

In this view you can see where your objects will be positioned on the page. Your margins are displayed (and any headers or footers – see section 8.2), and pictures, drawings, multiple columns, etc. are all displayed in their true position on the page.

Print Layout view is useful if you are working with headers and footers, altering your margins, working in columns, or are combining text and graphics on a page and wish to see how they will be placed relative to each other.

In some chapters in this book, Print Layout view will be recommended.

To change to Print Layout view:

1 Open the **View** menu

2 Choose **Print Layout**

Or

♦ Click the **Print Layout View** tool ▦ at the bottom left of the screen.

Show/hide white space

In Print Layout view you can show or hide the white space (top and bottom margin areas) at the top and the bottom of the page.

♦ Position the mouse pointer over the top or bottom edge of a page (it becomes the Hide White Space mouse pointer) and click.

♦ To show the white space again, position the mouse pointer between any two pages and click.

Summary

In this chapter we have discussed some of the basic skills you require to use Word efficiently.

You have learnt how to:

◆ Enter text.

◆ Spell and grammar check your document.

◆ Edit text.

◆ Move around your document using the mouse and the keyboard.

◆ Save your document.

◆ Use Print Preview and print your file.

◆ Close a document.

◆ Create a new document.

◆ Open an existing document.

◆ Select text using the mouse and the keyboard.

◆ Move and copy text within a document.

◆ Move and copy text to another document.

◆ Use the Office Clipboard

◆ Move and copy text using drag and drop techniques.

◆ View your document using Normal view and Print Layout view.

◆ Show or hide white space in Print Layout view.

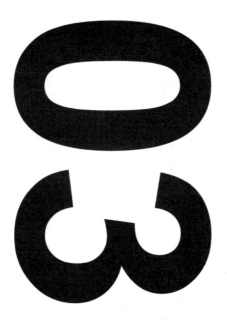

03

formatting

In this chapter you will learn

- how to apply font formatting
- some paragraph formatting options
- how to apply borders and shading
- what tabs and indents are used for
- about applying styles

Aims of this chapter

In this chapter we will look at some of the ways you can enhance your text to help give your documents more visual impact. We will discuss the font formatting and paragraph formatting options available.

3.1 Font formatting

One way of enhancing your text is to apply font formatting to it. The effects can be applied to individual characters in your document. You can underline them, increase their size, change their colour, or make them bold or italic.

Unless you specify otherwise, each character is formatted to use the Times New Roman font with a size of 10 points. (There are 72 points to an inch – this text, for example, is set in 11 point.)

The most commonly used font formatting options have tools on the Formatting toolbar – other options can be found in the Format, Font dialog box.

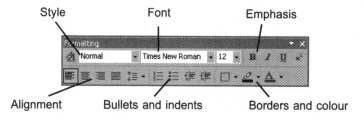

Style   Font   Emphasis

Alignment   Bullets and indents   Borders and colour

When applying font formatting you can either:

◆ Set the format then enter text.

Or

◆ Enter your text and then go back and apply the required formatting to it.

3.2 Bold, italic, underline and superscript

The bold, italic, underline and superscript formatting options are toggles – you switch them on and off in the same way. It is simplest to set them using the tools on the Formatting toolbar.

- To switch bold on or off, click the **Bold** tool.
- To switch italic on or off, click the *Italic* tool.
- To switch underline on or off, click the <u>Underline</u> tool.
- To switch superscript on or off, click.

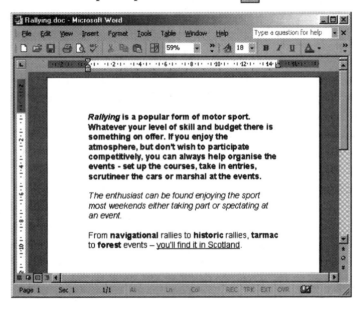

Keyboard shortcuts

You can switch Bold, Italic, Underline and Superscript on and off using the keyboard shortcuts [Ctrl] – [B], [Ctrl] – [I], [Ctrl] – [U] and [Shift] – [Ctrl] – [+].

To format text as you key it in:

1 Switch on the formatting option – bold, italic or underline

2 Enter your text

3 Switch the option off when you reach the end of the text

To format existing text:

1 Select the text you want to format (see section 2.9)

2 Click the appropriate tool to apply the formatting required

To remove formatting from text:

1 Select the text

2 Click the **Bold**, *Italic*, <u>Underline</u> or Superscript tool as necessary to remove the formatting

3.3 Font, size and colour

To change the font:

1 Click the drop-down arrow to the right of the **Font** tool on the Formatting toolbar

2 Scroll through the list of fonts until you see the font you want to use

3 Click on it

To change the size of font:

1 Click the drop-down arrow to the right of the **Font Size** tool on the Formatting toolbar

2 Scroll through the list of available sizes until you see the size you want to use

3 Click on it

To change the colour of font:

1 Click the drop-down arrow to the right of the **Font Color** tool on the Formatting toolbar to display the palette

2 Select the colour you want to use

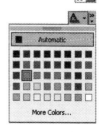

3.4 Highlight text

To highlight your text (the equivalent to using a marker pen on it) use the Highlight tool on the Formatting toolbar. The highlight you apply prints out – if you have a black and white printer, the colour will appear as grey shading behind your text.

To apply highlight to existing text:

1 Click the drop-down arrow to the right of the **Highlight** tool on the Formatting toolbar

2 Select the highlight colour you want to use

3 Click and drag over the text (the mouse pointer looks like the I-beam with a marker pen attached!)

4 Click the **Highlight** tool again to switch the function off

To remove highlight from existing text:

1 Select the text that has the highlight applied to it

2 Display the highlight options

3 Select **None**

Automatic word selection

To format a word, just position the insertion point anywhere inside it, then apply the font formatting. Word automatically formats the whole word surrounding the insertion point.

3.5 And yet more options

Explore the Font dialog box to find out what other font formatting options are available. Try some out on your text.

1 Open the **Format** menu and choose **Font**

2 Select a tab – **Font**, **Character Spacing** or **Text Effects**

3 Choose the effects you want – a preview of your selection is displayed in the Preview window

4 Click **OK** to apply the effects to your text, or **Cancel** to return to your document without making any changes

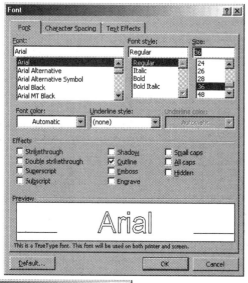

You can set all aspects of font formatting at once through the Font dialog box – and there are more effects here than on the toolbar

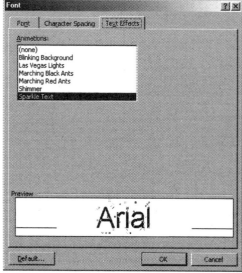

The Text Effects can liven up headlines and announcements

Default font

The default font is the one that is automatically used every time you create a new document – initially it is set to Times New Roman, size 10.

You can change these font options. Set the font options you require as your default using the tabs in the **Font** dialog box, and click the **Default...** button. You will be asked to confirm the change. Click **Yes** to do so, or **No** to cancel.

3.6 Paragraph formatting

Some formatting options are applied to complete paragraphs, regardless of whether the paragraph consists of a few words or several lines. A paragraph is created in Word each time you press [Enter]. The heading at the top of this text is a paragraph and this is a paragraph. Each time you press [**Enter**] you insert a *paragraph mark* into the document.

Paragraph formatting options include:

Alignment	Line spacing	Borders and shading
Bulleted lists	Numbered lists	Indents Tabs

Show/Hide non-printing characters

You can toggle the display of the paragraph marks in your document using the **Show/Hide** tool ¶ on the Standard toolbar. The paragraph marks are *non-printing* characters – they do not print out even if they are displayed on your screen.

Other non-printing characters, e.g. a dot for each space or an arrow for each Tab keypress, are also displayed on your screen.

Specifying paragraph formatting

When applying paragraph formatting to text you can either:

♦ Set the paragraph format then enter your text.

Or

♦ Enter your text and apply the paragraph formatting later.

The default paragraph formatting options (those normally used) give you a left-aligned paragraph, with single line spacing. If this is not the formatting you require you can change it.

To change the paragraph formatting of consecutive paragraphs, select them first, and then change the formatting.

Automatic paragraph selection

If you wish to apply paragraph formatting to an existing paragraph, just position the insertion point anywhere inside it, then apply the formatting.

To format paragraphs as you enter text:

1 Select the paragraph formatting options required – alignment (see section 3.7), line spacing (see section 3.8), etc.

2 Type in your text – each time you press [**Enter**], the paragraph formatting options you have set will carry forward with you to the next paragraph

3 Press [**Enter**] at the end of the last paragraph that you want the formatting applied to

4 Select the next formatting option required

To format existing paragraphs:

1 Select the paragraph(s) you want to format (see section 2.9)

2 Specify the formatting

3.7 Alignment

The alignment of your paragraphs can be left, right, centre or justified (see the examples on the next page). The default alignment is left, where the text is flush with the left margin and has a ragged right-hand edge.

To centre align

◆ Click the **Centre** tool ▦ or use the shortcut [**Ctrl**]-[**E**].

To justify

◆ Click the **Justify** tool ▦ or press [**Ctrl**]-[**J**].

To right align

◆ Click the **Align Right** tool ▦ or press [**Ctrl**]-[**R**].

To left align

◆ Click the **Align Left** tool ▦ or press [**Ctrl**]-[**L**].

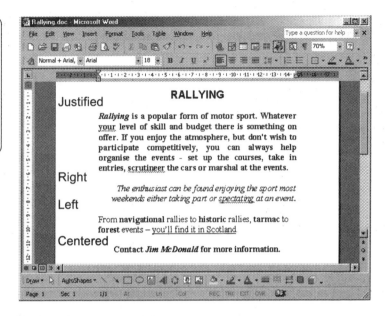

3.8 Line spacing

Initially, your line spacing is set to single. You can set different spacing using the Line Spacing tool.

1   Select the text you wish to change
2   Click the drop-down arrow beside the **Line Spacing** tool
3   Click on the Line Spacing option required

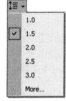

To apply the most recently used line spacing option, simply click the Line Spacing tool (not the drop-down arrow beside it).

If you wish to set line spacing to a measurement other than those listed, click **More...** and specify your requirements in the **Line Spacing** field in the **Format Paragraph** box (you can also access this dialog box from the **Format** menu).

Line spacing options

♦   **Single**   Accommodates the largest font in the line, and adds some extra space – how much depends upon the font.

♦   **1½**   1½ times that of single.

- **Double**   Double that of single.
- **At Least Minimum**   Word can adjust to accommodate larger font sizes and graphics. Set the value in the **At:** field.
- **Exactly**   Fixed line spacing. Set the value in the **At:** field.
- **Multiple**   Increased or decreased by a percentage, e.g. 1.5 would increase the spacing by 50% (the same as 1½ line spacing) 1.8 would increase the spacing by 80%. The default is 3. Set the value in the **At:** field.

Keyboard shortcuts

The keyboard shortcuts are: [Ctrl] – [2] for double spacing; [Ctrl] – [5] for 1½ line spacing; [Ctrl] – [1] for single spacing.

Spacing before and after paragraphs

You can also control the amount of spacing that appears before and after a paragraph in the **Format Paragraphs** dialog box. This option is useful if you wish to leave a space between paragraphs without having to press [**Enter**] twice.

1 Open the **Format** menu and choose **Paragraph**

2 Set the amount of spacing **Before** and/or **After** the selected paragraph(s)

3 Click **OK**

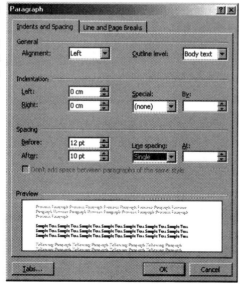

3.9 Borders and shading

Borders and shading are text or paragraph formatting options that can be very useful when it comes to emphasizing areas in your document.

To place a border around your text or paragraph(s):

1 Select the text or paragraph(s)

2 Click the drop-down arrow by the **Borders** tool to display the Borders toolbar

3 Select a border from the options

To remove a border from your paragraph(s):

1 Select the text or paragraph(s) you want to remove borders from

2 Display the Borders toolbar

3 Click the **No Border** tool

There are format options on the Tables and Borders toolbar. This can be switched on and off using the **Tables and Borders** tool 🔳 on the Standard toolbar.

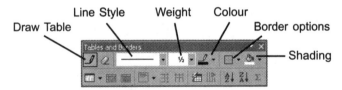

When this toolbar appears, the Draw Table tool is initially selected – switch it off by clicking on it (tables are discussed in Chapter 7).

To customize your borders:

1 Choose the **Line Style**, **Weight** and **Colour** required

2 Click the **Draw Table** tool (to switch it off)

3 Select the text, paragraph(s) as necessary

4 Pick the border type required from the Border options

There are more options in the Borders and Shading dialog box. You can apply a border to all 4 sides (an outside border) using the Box, Shadow or 3-D setting.

1 From the **Format** menu choose **Borders and Shading…**
2 Select the **Borders** tab
3 Choose a **Setting** from the list – **Box, Shadow** or 3-D
4 Pick a line style from the **Style** list
5 Select the **Color** and the line **Width** (measured in points)
6 Click **OK**

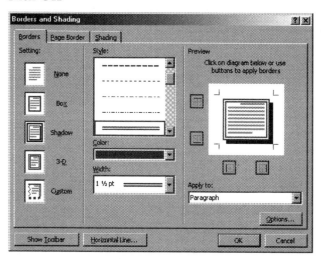

To switch individual borders (left, right, top or bottom) on and off, click the border tools in the Preview window, or the lines around the edges of the example in the Preview window.

If you choose **Custom** border from the **Setting** list, you can specify different borders for different sides of the selected area.

1 From the **Format** menu choose **Borders and Shading…**
2 Select the **Borders** tab
3 Choose the **Custom** setting from the list on the left
4 Pick a line style from the **Style** list
5 Select the colour and the line width required
6 Click on the appropriate button or line in the **Preview** panel
7 Repeat steps 4–6 until you've specified all the borders
8 Click **OK**

Horizontal line

In addition to the dialog box options, there are some special horizontal line designs to choose from. These can be used in any document, and are very effective on Web pages.

1 From the **Format** menu choose **Borders and Shading...**

2 Select the **Borders** tab

3 Click **Horizontal Line...**

4 Select a line

5 Click **OK**

Shading

You can use the **Shading** tool on the Tables and Borders toolbar to add shading to your text or paragraph(s).

1 Select the text or paragraph(s) you wish to add shading to

2 Use **Format > Borders and Shading...** and go to the **Shading** tab to apply a particular type of shading e.g. diagonal or horizontal lines

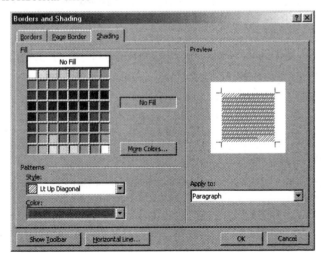

Or

3 If you just want to set the colour, click the down arrow beside the **Shading** tool and pick a colour from the palette

The text in the following example has a top and bottom border on the heading, black shading on the middle paragraph, and an outside border around the last paragraph.

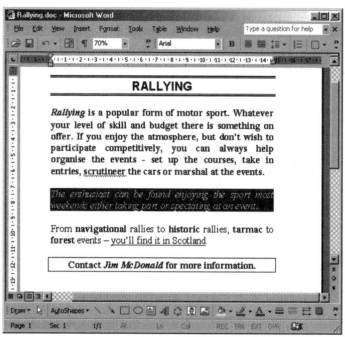

Black and white

The higher the percentage of the grey fill colour chosen in the Borders and Shading dialog box, the harder it gets to read your text through it (unless you change your font colour). However, if you choose black, Word automatically displays the text as white.

3.10 Bulleted lists

You can easily add bullets automatically to your paragraphs.

To add bullets as you enter your text:

1 Click the Bullets tool 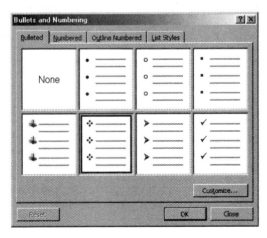 on the Formatting toolbar to switch the bullets on

2 Type in your text

3 Press [**Enter**] to create a new paragraph – it is automatically given a bullet

4 Press [**Enter**] twice, without entering any text, and the bullets are switched off

To add bullets to – or remove them from – existing paragraphs:

1 Select the paragraphs

2 Click the **Bullets** tool to toggle them on or off

To change the bullet style:

1 Select the paragraphs you want bulleted

2 Open the **Format** menu and choose **Bullets and Numbering**

3 Select the **Bulleted** tab in the dialog box

4 Choose a bullet from those displayed in the **Bullets and Numbering** dialog box

5 Click **OK**

Customized bullets

1 Select the paragraphs you want bulleted
2 From the **Format** menu choose **Bullets and Numbering**
3 Select the **Bulleted** tab in the dialog box
4 Choose a bullet from those displayed
5 Click the **Customize** button

• To change the size or colour of the bullet, click the **Font...** button, set the options in the Font dialog box and click **OK**.

• To get a new bullet character, click the **Character...** button to open the **Symbol** dialog box. Change the character set through the **Font** list, and select a character, then click **OK**.

6 Click **OK** in the **Customize Bulleted List** dialog box

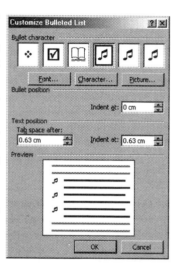

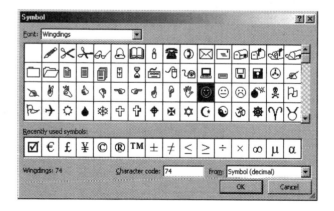

Picture bullets

1 Start as for a normal bullet, then click **Picture...** on the **Customize Bulleted List** dialog box

2 Select a bullet from the dialog box

3 Click **OK**

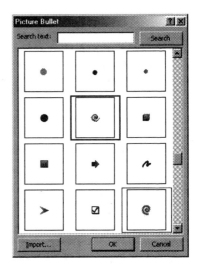

Numbered lists

You can number your paragraphs in much the same way as you apply bullets to them – just use the **Numbering** tool.

Word keeps your numbering up to date as you edit your list. If you add extra paragraphs into your list, delete some, move or copy them, Word will automatically renumber the list.

To customize the numbering style and format, open the **Bullets and Numbering** dialog box. From the **Numbered** tab you can specify that Word restarts numbering, or continues from the previous list.

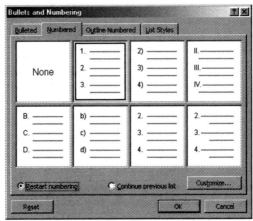

You can customize the position and appearance of the number:

1 Click the **Customize...** button

2 Customize your number format, style and positions as required.

• Watch the preview window to see the effect that your changes will have.

3 Click **OK**

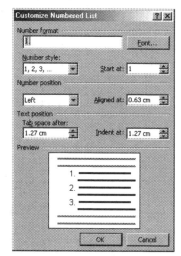

If your working through a document, switching numbering on and off, a Smart Tag will appear automatically so that you can specify how you wish your numbering to proceed, or display the dialog box so you can customize your numbering.

3.11 Indents

Paragraphs normally run the full width of your typing line – from the left to the right margin. As you enter text, it extends along the line until it reaches the right margin and then automatically wraps to the next line, unless you press [**Enter**].

In fact your text actually runs from the left *indent marker* to the right *indent marker* (not from left to right margin) – but the indent markers are flush with the margins unless you set them differently.

If you want to leave some white space between your text and the margin you can move the indent markers inwards. Paragraphs that do not have text running from margin to margin are indented paragraphs.

You can change the position of the indents in the Paragraph dialog box, or drag the indent markers into position on the ruler (see page 61).

To change the indents using the Paragraph dialog box:

1 Open the **Format** menu and choose **Paragraph**

2 Select the **Indents and Spacing** tab

3 Set the left and/or right indent required in the Left and Right fields in the Indentation area of the dialog box – this will be applied to all the lines in your paragraph

4 Special indent effects – hanging or first line only – can be specified in the **Special** list field

5 Use the Preview window to see the effect you are creating

6 Click **OK** to confirm your settings

Some of the effects are illustrated here.

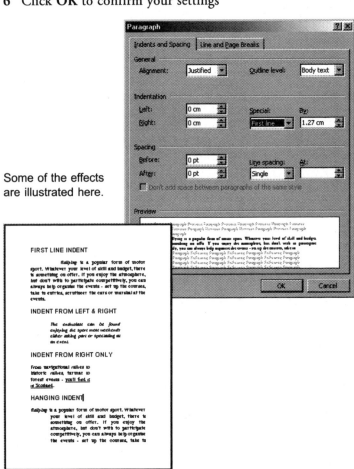

Make life easy

Don't be tempted to push text along each line in a paragraph using spaces or tabs, or cut lines short by pressing **[Enter]**, to get an indented effect. Such spaces, tabs or paragraph ends can result in a lot of extra work and unnecessary frustration if you need to insert or delete text later.

Using the horizontal ruler

Indent markers

You can also use the ruler to set your indents. The ruler must be displayed along the top of your text area – if it's not, open the **View** menu and choose **Ruler**. The indent markers are the two triangles and the small rectangle below them at the left edge of the ruler, and the small triangle at the right.

* To set the indent, drag the appropriate indent marker along the ruler to the correct position.

To improve accuracy when setting indents using the ruler, you can display the exact position of your indent on the ruler as you drag it along.

* Hold the [**Alt**] key down while you click and drag.

Style button

You can also set the left indents using the style button to the left of the horizontal ruler.

* Click the button until the indent you require is displayed – ▼ for first line indent or ▣ for all lines except the first – then click on the lower edge of the ruler where you want to set your indent.

The ruler's measurements can be in inches, centimetres, milli-metres, points or picas. To change the units, choose **Options** from the **Tools** menu and set the units on the **General** tab.

3.12 Tabs

Tabs are used to align text vertically. If you wanted a list of names and phone numbers you could use tabs to align the columns.

Each time you press the [**Tab**] key, the insertion point jumps forward to the next tab position. The default tabs are set every 1.27cm (½ inch) – the small dark grey marks along the bottom edge of the ruler indicate their positions. They have left alignment – when you enter your text or numbers the left edge is at the tab position.

Tabs can be aligned to the left, right, centre, or decimal point, or draw a bar.

Alignment	Effect	Possible usage
Left	Left edge at tab	Any text or numbers
Right	Right edge at tab	Text, or numbers you want to line up on the unit
Centre	Centred under tab	Anything
Decimal	Decimal point under tab	Figures you want to line up on the decimal point
Bar	Vertical line at tab	To draw a vertical line between columns

If you need to use tabs and the pre-set ones are not what you require, you must set tabs at the positions you need them.

Using the ruler

To set a tab:

1 Select the type of tab – click the style button to the left of the ruler until you've got the alignment option required – ▣ **Left**, ▣ **Centre**, ▣ **Right**, ▣ **Decimal** or ▣ **Bar**

2 Point to the lower half of the ruler and click – the tab is set

To move a tab:

♦ Drag it along the ruler to its correct position.

To delete a tab:

◆ Drag it *down* off the ruler, and drop it.

To set tabs in the Tabs dialog box

1 From the **Format** menu choose **Tabs**

2 Enter the **Tab stop position**

3 Pick the **Alignment**

4 Click **Set**

5 Repeat until all your tabs are set

6 Click **OK**

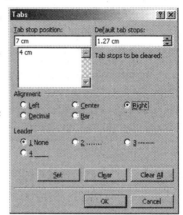

Leader characters

Leader characters are useful to guide the eye along the line when your columns are not close together. They can be set through the **Tabs** dialog box. Simply choose one before you click **Set**.

In the example below, a centre tab was set at 7.25cm for the heading *newsletter,* and a right tab was set at 14.5cm for the date. The issue number is at the left margin.

Underneath the paragraph that says *contents*, the centre tab was removed, by dragging it off the Ruler, and a leader character added to the tab at 14.5cm (in the **Tabs** dialog box, select that tab, choose a Leader style and click **Set**).

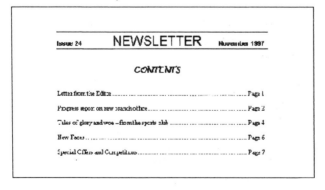

3.13   Format Painter

If you need to apply the same formatting to different pieces of text throughout your document, you could use the Format Painter to 'paint' the formatting onto your text.

1   Select some text with the formatting you want to use

2   Click the **Format Painter** tool 🔲

3   Click and drag over the text to 'paint' on the formatting

If you want to paint the formats onto several separate pieces of text, lock the Format Painter on by double-clicking on it. When you have finished, click the tool again to unlock it.

3.14   Formatting Task Panes

Styles and Formatting Task Pane

The Styles and Formatting Task Pane can be used to apply formatting to your text. To display (or hide) the Task Pane click the **Styles and Formatting** 🔲 tool on the Formatting toolbar.

Formatting options that are currently in use, and Styles that are available to the current document (see Chapter 6), are displayed in the Task Pane. Each time you apply new formatting combinations to your text, an entry will appear in the formatting list. You can then apply the same formatting to other text by selecting it from the Task Pane. Using the Task Pane in this way can make formatting quicker and make it easier to keep your formatting consistent throughout your document.

As the contents of the Task pane reflect the formatting options used in the active document, they may vary considerably from file to file.

To use the Task Pane formatting:

1   Scroll through the document in the left pane

2   Select the text that you wish to format

3   Pick the formatting that you wish to apply from the list in the Task Pane

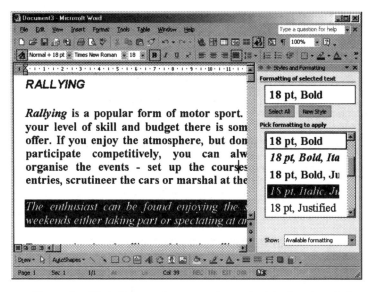

- Close the Task Pane when you have finished using it by clicking 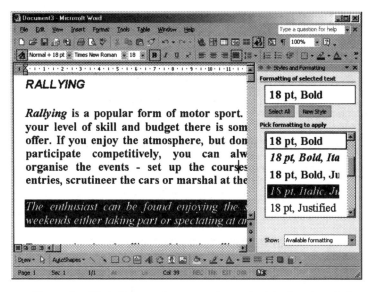.

Reveal Formatting Task Pane

If you wish to check the formatting of existing text, or compare the formatting of one bit of text with another, the Reveal Formatting Task Pane will be useful.

- To display the **Reveal Formatting** Task Pane, open the **Format** menu and choose **Reveal Formatting**.

With this Task Pane displayed you can select any text in your document and check the font and paragraph formatting options that have been applied to it.

If you wish to compare the formatting of text in one part of your document with that in another:

1 Select the text that you wish to compare with

2 Click the **Compare to another selection** checkbox

3 Select the text that you wish to compare

Information regarding how the selections compare will be displayed in the Task Pane.

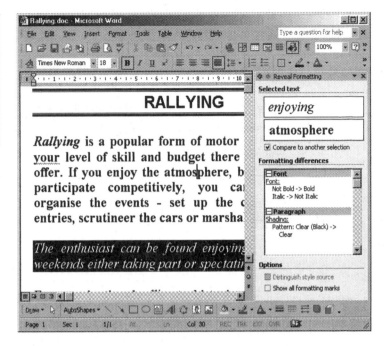

The formatting on the left of the -> is the formatting that has been applied to the text identified in the upper box. The formatting on the right of the -> is the formatting that has been applied to the text in identified in the lower box.

At the top left of the Styles and Formatting Task Pane are a couple of arrows pointing left and right. These arrows can be used to switch between the Styles and Formatting Task Pane and the Reveal Formatting Task Pane.

Summary

We have discussed many of the formatting options in Word in this chapter. You have been introduced to:

- Formatting text to make it bold, underlined or in italics.
- Changing the font style, size and colour.
- Highlighting text.
- The Font dialog box.
- Paragraph formatting techniques.
- Non-printing characters.
- Alignment and line spacing options.
- Applying borders, shading and lines to paragraphs.
- Creating bulleted and numbered lists.
- Customizing the bullets in your list.
- Indenting text from the left and right margins.
- Aligning text with tabs.
- Format Painter.
- Styles and Formatting Task Pane.
- Reveal Formatting Task Pane.

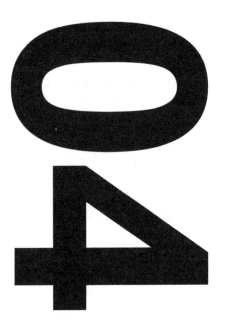

04

sections and page layout

In this chapter you will learn

- about sections
- how to change margins and orientation
- some multi-page layouts
- how to use newspaper columns
- about page border options

Aims of this chapter

In this chapter we will discuss sections and some of the page layout options in Word. You will learn how to change the layout of the whole document, or just part of it. We will discuss margins, page orientation, columns and borders.

4.1 Sections

Sections are used in every Word document. Up until now, the documents we have looked at have consisted of one section only.

If you look at the left of the Status bar, `Page 1    Sec 1        1/8` you will see information about the current position of the insertion point within your document. In this case, the insertion point is currently in Page 1, Section 1 of an 8-page document.

Many documents contain only one section – others may have several. You may need to divide a document up into sections for a variety of reasons:

- Part of the document has a different *orientation* – i.e. some of the pages are landscape, others are portrait.

- Some of the pages may need different margin settings.

- You might want to set up a page to display a different number of columns on different parts of the page – perhaps for a newsletter layout.

When you change a layout feature and apply it from **This point forward** in a dialog box, Word automatically inserts a section break for you. You can also insert breaks as needed using the **Break** dialog box.

To insert a section break:

1 Choose **Break** from the **Insert** menu

2 Select a section break option

3 Click **OK**

Section break options

Next Page	Inserts a section break at the insertion point and starts the next section at the top of the next page
Continuous	Inserts a section break at the insertion point, and starts the next section immediately
Even Page	Inserts a section break and starts the next section on the next even numbered page
Odd Page	Inserts a section break and starts the next section on the next odd numbered page

• You can also insert page breaks in the Break dialog box – page breaks are discussed fully in Chapter 8, *Multi-page documents*.

Section breaks are always displayed in Normal view. You can display them in Print Layout view if you show your non-printing characters.

Once you have inserted a section break, you can format each section individually. You can tell which section your insertion point is in by checking the section indicator on the Status bar.

To change the formatting of a section:

1 Place the insertion point within the section
2 Make the changes required
    • Margins (see section 4.2 below)
    • Orientation (see section 4.2 below)
    • Number of columns (see section 4.4 below)
    • Page borders (see section 4.5 below)
3 Click **OK**

To remove a section break:

1 Select the section break (show non-printing characters if necessary)
2 Press [**Delete**]

When you remove a section break, the section that was above the break adopts the formatting of the section that was below.

4.2 Margins and orientation

When you create a blank document the margins are automatically set at 1 inch (2.54cm) top and bottom, 1.25 inch (3.17cm) right and left. You can change the margins for all or part of the document.

Using the Page Setup dialog box

The easiest way to change margins is through the Page Setup.

1 Open the **File** menu and choose **Page Setup...**

2 Select the **Margins** tab

3 Edit the margin fields as necessary

4 Set the orientation required

5 Use the **Apply to:** field to specify the area of the document you want to apply the changes to. Select:

◆ **This section** to change the settings just for the section the insertion point is in (if there are several sections).

◆ **Whole document** if you want every page on your document to take on the new settings.

◆ **This point forward** to change the setting from the insertion point onwards – a section break is inserted into your document automatically when you choose this option.

6 Click **OK**

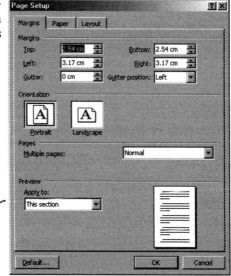

Select the area to be formatted

Using the ruler

You can also change your margins using the ruler. You must be in Print Layout view if you want to change the margins using this method.

In Print Layout view, the dark grey area on the ruler indicates the margin area – the white area shows the typing area.

The top and bottom margin areas are displayed when you are at the top and bottom of the page respectively.

To change the margins using the ruler:

1 Go into **Print Layout** view (if necessary)

2 Point to where the dark grey and white areas meet – the pointer changes to a double-headed arrow, and a prompt tells you which margin you are over (it can be tricky getting the left margin prompt as the indents are in the same area)

3 Click and drag the margin to its new position

If you want to see the exact measurements for the margins and the distance between them, hold [**Alt**] down as you drag the margin.

When you change your margins using the ruler, they will affect only the section your insertion point is in – or the whole document if there is only one section.

4.3 Multiple page options

If you are going to bind your document, you need to set a 'gutter margin' to allow for the binding. You can set a gutter margin for the left or top of the page.

If your binding method is going to take up 1.25cm down the left edge (or top) of your pages, set the gutter to 1.25cm. This amount will be left at the edge before the left (or top) margin is calculated – the distance between the margins is reduced automatically to allow for the gutter.

There are a number of options to choose from in Page Setup if you have a multi-page document.

◆ **Normal** – is normal!

◆ **Mirror Margins** – useful if you want to print a document double-sided, then bind it. Set your gutter (if required), then select Mirror Margins from the Pages options. If you have set a gutter margin, the Left and Right fields change to Outside and Inside – the gutter is on the inside.

* **2 pages per sheet** – prints 2 pages on each sheet of paper. The paper can be portrait or landscape orientation.

* **Book fold** – If you wish to produce a booklet, specify the page setup by choosing Book fold *before* you begin to enter your text/graphics. If you don't you may find that you have to reposition objects and reformat text to get the layout required. The paper orientation is automatically set to landscape (if you haven't already specified this) and the left and right margins change to outside and inside margins. You must specify the number of pages that will be in your booklet in the **Sheets per booklet:** field. Two pages are printed on one side of the paper.

4.4 Columns

Most documents have the text in one column, running across the page from margin to margin. If you create leaflets, newsletters or advertising 'fliers', you may want your text to appear in several columns across your page.

If you want a different number of columns on different parts of a page, you must divide the page up using *Continuous* section breaks.

To insert a continuous section break:

1 Place the insertion point where you want the section break

2 Choose **Break** from the **Insert** menu

3 Select **Continuous** and click **OK**

You must then set the number of columns required in each section.

1 Place the insertion point in the section you want to edit

2 Click the **Columns** tool and drag over the number of columns required

Or

3 Open the **Format** menu and choose **Columns**

4 Specify the number of columns required – you can have up to 10 (portrait orientation) or 16 (landscape orientation) on A4 size paper if you use the **Number of columns** field

5 Select any other options required, e.g. **Line between** (columns)

• If you don't want your columns all the same width, deselect the **Equal column width** checkbox and set the **Width** and **Spacing** (distance between columns) options as required.

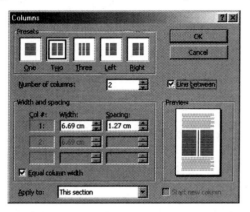

6 Click **OK**

When you type your text into a page that has multiple columns, the text flows down to the bottom of the first column on the page, then wraps to the top of the next column. It then fills the second column, then wraps to the next one and so on.

You can force a column break if you don't want the text to run to the bottom of the page.

To insert a manual column break:

1 Place the insertion point where you want to insert a column break

2 Open the **Insert** menu and choose **Break…**

3 Select **Column break**

4 Click **OK**

• **The keyboard shortcut is [Shift] – [Ctrl] – [Enter]**

The example at the top of page 75 has a continuous section break inserted after the heading. Section 1 is set to display one column – this allows the heading to run across the whole page.

Section 2 is formatted to display 2 columns. The text has wrapped automatically at the bottom of the first column and flowed to the top of column 2.

You can find out how to insert a picture in Chapter 11.

4.5 Page borders

If you want to add a special effect to a page, you might like to have a look through the Page Border options. Page borders can be very effective on menus, newsletters, programmes, invitations, etc.

To apply a page border:

1 Choose **Borders and Shading…** from the **Format** menu
2 Select the **Page Border** tab
3 Select the border style – either use the basic line styles, or try out the **Art** options
4 Click **OK**

Summary

In this chapter we have discussed:

◆ Sections.

◆ Margins.

◆ Orientation.

◆ Multi-page layouts.

◆ Columns.

◆ Page borders.

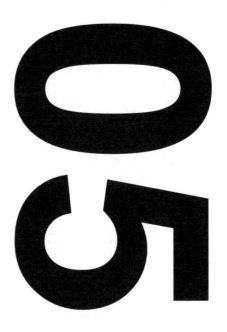

05

automating tasks

In this chapter you will learn

- about AutoText
- how to manage your AutoCorrect entries
- some wizard ways of creating documents!

Aims of this chapter

In this chapter we will consider some ways in which you can automate your work in Word. We will discuss AutoText, AutoCorrect, AutoComplete and some of the wizards.

5.1 AutoText

How often do you type the same text or insert the same picture (see Chapter 11) into a document? It could be your name and address, a department name, a circulation list, clauses in contracts or a company logo. If you retype the same text often, you should consider making the text into an AutoText entry. You can then insert the text with a few keystrokes or mouse clicks – even if it is several paragraphs long.

If you use AutoText entries a lot, you could display the AutoText toolbar (see 13.1).

Creating an AutoText

To create an AutoText entry:

1 Select the text or picture you want to make into an AutoText entry – include the paragraph mark at the end if you want the paragraph formatting saved with the entry

2 Click **New...** on the AutoText toolbar

Or

* Open the **Insert** menu, choose **AutoText**, then **New** (or press [**Alt**]-[**F3**]).

3 Either accept the name suggested or edit it as required

4 Click **OK**

Insert AutoText

If you know the name of the AutoText entry:

1 Position the insertion point where you want the AutoText entry to appear

2 Type in the AutoText entry name (don't put a space at the end of it)

3 Press [**F3**]

If you know the category but not the name of an AutoText entry:

1 Choose a category in the **All Entries** list (on AutoText toolbar)

Or

◆ Open the **Insert** menu and choose **AutoText**, then choose a category.

2 Click on the entry required

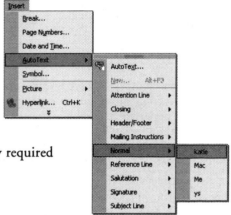

If you don't know the category or name of the AutoText entry:

1 Click **AutoText** on the AutoText toolbar

Or

2 Open the **Insert** menu, select **AutoText** then **AutoText...**

◆ Browse through the list and select the entry required from the **AutoText** tab in the **AutoCorrect** dialog box

3 Click **Insert**

AutoComplete

You may have noticed that Word automatically suggests your AutoText entry as you enter the AutoText name into your document.

This is the AutoComplete tip. If you want to insert the entry, press [**Enter**] or [**F3**] when the tip appears. If you don't want to insert the AutoText entry, ignore the tip and keep typing.

You can switch this feature on and off on the **AutoText** tab in the **AutoCorrect** dialog box. Select or deselect the **Show**

AutoComplete suggestions checkbox at the top of the dialog box as required.

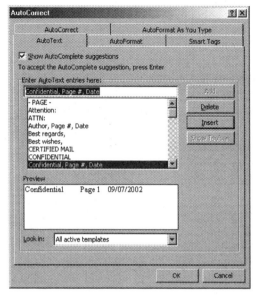

To delete an AutoText entry:

1 Display the **AutoText** tab in the **AutoCorrect** dialog box

2 Select the entry to be deleted from the list

3 Click **Delete**

To redefine (edit) an AutoText entry:

1 Insert the AutoText entry into your document

2 Make the changes required – e.g. add, delete, format

3 Select the edited AutoText entry in your document

4 Press [**Alt**]-[**F3**]

5 Enter the original AutoText entry name

6 Click **OK**

7 At the prompt, click **Yes** to replace the old version with the new

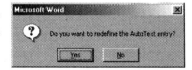

To rename an AutoText entry:

1 From the **Tools** menu, choose **Templates and Add-ins**

2 Click **Organizer**

3 Select the **AutoText** tab

4 Choose the entry you want to rename from the **In** list

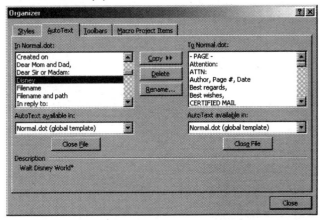

5 Click **Rename**

6 Enter the new name for the entry in the **Rename** dialog box

7 Click **OK**

8 Click **Close**

5.2 The Spike

The Spike is a special AutoText entry that you can use to re-arrange the text and graphics within your document. It is a container into which you can collect text and graphics from non-adjacent locations in your document. Once you have collected them, you can insert the contents of the Spike wherever you wish. You may find that there are times that you can use the Spike to save you several cut and paste operations.

The text and graphics are added to the Spike in the order you want them to reappear in your document. When you add an item to the Spike, it is deleted from your document. You then empty the contents of the Spike at the desired location.

To add items to the Spike:

1 Select the first item required

2 Press [**Ctrl**]-[**F3**]

3 Repeat steps 1 and 2 until you've collected everything required

To empty the contents of the Spike into your document:

1 Position the insertion point where you want the contents of
the Spike to appear

2 Press [**Ctrl**]-[**Shift**]-[**F3**]

You must empty the Spike before you start building up a new
group of items – if you don't empty it, anything you add is
appended to what's already there.

However, you can insert the contents of the Spike into your
document without emptying the Spike if you wish.

To insert the contents of the Spike without emptying it:

1 Position the insertion point where you want the contents of
the Spike to appear

2 Display the **AutoText** tab – click the tool on the AutoText
toolbar

3 Select **Spike** from the list – a preview will appear in the
Preview window

4 Click **Insert**

5.3 AutoText field

If you are adding the same text many times to a long document – a clause to a contract or disclaimer to a legal document
– and the contents of the clause or disclaimer have not yet
been finalized, you can still use an AutoText entry.

When the wording in the clause or disclaimer becomes final, it
would be more efficient to have the AutoText entry updated
automatically throughout your document, rather than you have
to go to each occurrence and delete the old version and insert
the new one. It is possible to do this if you enter your AutoText
entry as a *field* rather than a normal AutoText entry. A field is
a placeholder or code that is used to indicate where the data

should appear, but the actual contents of the placeholder can be updated automatically.

You will meet many different types of field in Word. An AutoText field can be updated automatically if the contents of the AutoText entry change – which might save you a lot of work in some cases.

To insert an AutoText entry as a field:

1 Place the insertion point where you want the AutoText field to appear

2 Open the **Insert** menu and choose **Field...**

3 Select **Links and References** in the **Categories** list

4 Choose **AutoText** in the **Field names** list

5 Select the Auto-Text entry you wish to enter as a field

6 Click **OK** to close the Field dialog box

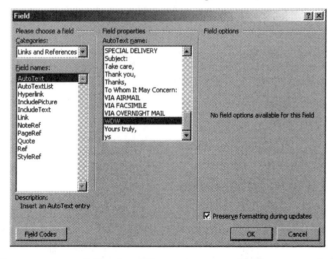

The contents of the AutoText entry are added to your document as a field.

If the contents of the AutoText entry are edited, you will need to update the AutoText fields so that they show the modified version of the AutoText entry. You can update your AutoText fields individually, collectively or when you print.

Redefine the contents of the AutoText entry as described in section 5.1 above. The AutoText fields *will not* pick up the edited version of the AutoText entry automatically.

To update an individual Auto Text field:

1 Click anywhere within the AutoText field you wish to update

2 Press [F9]

To update all your Auto Text fields at the same time:

1 Select the whole document – press [**Ctrl**]-[**A**]

2 Press [**F9**]

3 Deselect the text

To update your Auto Text fields when you print a document:

1 Open the **Tools** menu and choose **Options**

2 Select the **Print** tab

3 Select the **Update Fields** checkbox on the **Print** tab

4 Click **OK**

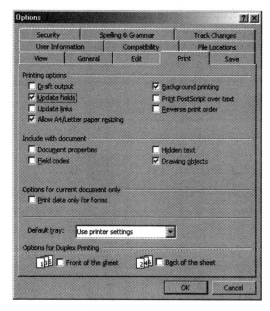

Your fields will be updated the next time you print your document.

5.4 AutoCorrect

The AutoCorrect feature helps you correct your typing errors quickly. Some 'typos' are very common – Word recognizes many of them and corrects them automatically. If your type in 'hte' you will find that Word changes it to 'the', or when you type 'adn' it becomes 'and'. If you start typing a new sentence without using an initial capital on the first word, Word will fix it!

If you tend to make specific typing errors that Word doesn't recognize – you can easily add these to Word's recognized list.

To display the list of AutoCorrect entries already set up:

1 Open the **Tools** menu

2 Choose **AutoCorrect Options...**

The dialog box shows the list of entries, and the AutoCorrect options that are selected.

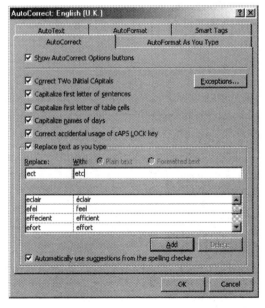

To add an entry to the list:

1 Open the **Tools** menu and choose **AutoCorrect Options...**

2 On the **AutoCorrect** tab, enter the text you want to be automatically replaced in the **Replace** field

3 Key in the text you want to replace it with in the **With** field

4 Click **Add**

5 Click **OK**

To delete an entry from the list:

1 Open the **Tools** menu and choose **AutoCorrect Options...**

2 Select the entry you wish to delete

3 Click **Delete**

4 Click **OK**

To redefine (replace) an entry in the list:

1 Open the **Tools** menu and choose **AutoCorrect Options...**

2 Select the entry you want to redefine

3 Edit the **With** field as required

4 Click **Replace**

5 At the **Redefine** prompt, click **Yes**

6 Click **OK**

Spellcheck and Autocorrect

You will notice an AutoCorrect button appears in the Spelling and Grammar dialog box when you spell check your document.

To add your error and correction to the AutoCorrect list:

1 Select the correct word from the suggestion list, or edit your error

2 Click **AutoCorrect**

5.5 Document wizards

Up until now, any documents we have created have been based on the Blank Document template – which gives a blank A4 sized sheet on which to enter your text.

We will consider other template options later, but, for the time being, if you want to create a letter, memo, fax or résumé document, you might like to try a **wizard** to step you through the process of setting up the document.

We'll try a couple of the document wizards. This first one is for a memo:

1 Open the **File** menu and choose **New...**

2 Select **New from Template**, **General Templates** from the **New Document Task Pane**

3 At the **Templates** dialog box, select the **Memos** tab and click on the **Memo Wizard**

4 Choose **Document** from the **Create New** options and click **OK**

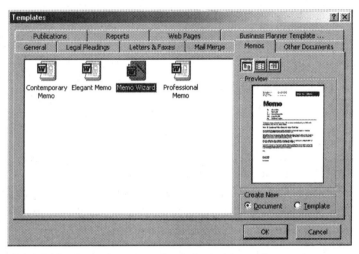

5 Work through the Wizard, clicking **Next** after each step

6 When you reach the final step, click **Finish**

◆ At the **cc** field, 'Click here' and type in details if necessary – otherwise 'Click here' and press [**Delete**] to get rid of the prompt.

◆ If you included a **priority** field – click and type in your priority message.

◆ To type in the body of your memo – 'Click here' as prompted, and type.

The headers and footers on each page are inserted automatically with the detail you selected at the Header/Footer step in the Wizard.

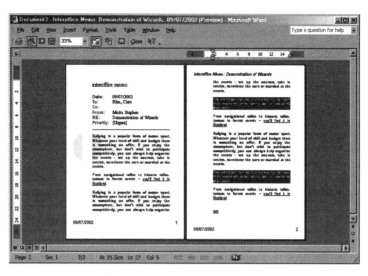

This time try out the **Letter Wizard**.

1 Open the **File** menu and choose **New…**

2 Select **New from Template, General Templates** from the **New Document Task Pane**

3 Select the **Letters & Faxes** tab

4 Choose **Letter Wizard** then **Document** from the **Create New Options** and click **OK**

5 At the prompt, select **Send one letter**

6 Complete each step of the wizard as required

7 Click **Finish** when you have reached the end

8 Specify your label and/or envelope requirements

9 Select the text under the salutation, delete it and type in the body of your letter

If you need to edit any of the elements automatically inserted by the Letter Wizard:

1 Open the **Tools** menu and select **Letters and Mailing**

2 Choose **Letter Wizard…**

3 Select the tab that contains the element(s) you wish to edit

4 Make the changes as required

5   Click **OK**

If you think the document wizards would be useful, try out the Fax Wizard and the Résumé Wizard. Experiment with the options available until you find a style that appeals to you.

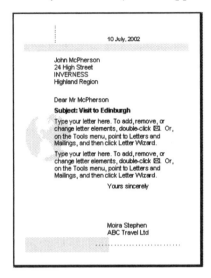

10 July, 2002

John McPherson
24 High Street
INVERNESS
Highland Region

Dear Mr McPherson

Subject: Visit to Edinburgh

Type your letter here. To add, remove, or change letter elements, double-click ⊠. Or, on the Tools menu, point to Letters and Mailings, and then click Letter Wizard.

Type your letter here. To add, remove, or change letter elements, double-click ⊠. Or, on the Tools menu, point to Letters and Mailings, and then click Letter Wizard.

Yours sincerely

Moira Stephen
ABC Travel Ltd

Summary

In this chapter we have discussed some options that can help improve your efficiency by automating tasks. We have discussed how you can:

+ Create, use and manage AutoText entries.

+ Use the Spike to collect text up before inserting it at a new location.

+ Automate the updating of AutoText entries by using AutoText fields.

+ Add, replace and delete AutoCorrect entries.

+ Create a memo using a Memo Wizard.

+ Create a letter using a Letter Wizard.

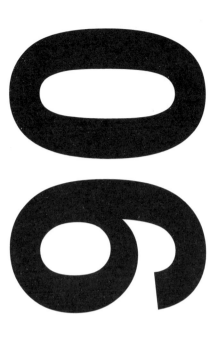

06

styles

In this chapter you will learn

- about the styles that come with Word
- how to create your own styles
- how to manage your styles
- about the Style Gallery

Aims of this chapter

In this chapter we will discuss styles. You'll find out why styles are important (and very useful). You can use the styles set up in Word or modify them to suit your own requirements. You can also create your own styles – it's up to you.

6.1 Putting on the style

What is a style?

A style is simply a collection of formatting options that you name. There are two kinds of style:

♦ Character styles – where the formatting options are taken from those in the Font dialog box.

♦ Paragraph styles – where the formatting options can be a combination of font and paragraph formatting.

Why should you use styles?

Speed – Once you've collected your formatting options into a style, you can then apply the style to your text, rather than apply each formatting option individually. If you have more than a couple of formatting options stored in your style, it is usually quicker to apply a style than apply each formatting option individually.

Consistency – If you collect the formatting options you want to use into a style, then apply the style to your text and paragraphs as required, the formatting throughout your document will be more consistent.

♦ Word's Heading styles 1–9 make it easier to work with long documents. They are used in Outline view (section 8.7) and when generating a Table of Contents (section 8.9).

You've been using styles since you started using Word – but you probably didn't notice. The formatting that your font and paragraph have are determined by a style called *Normal*.

The default Normal style is a paragraph style that is left aligned and in single line spacing. The characters are formatted using the Times New Roman font, size 10 (unless you've edited it).

The **Style** box Normal on the Formatting toolbar tells you the style that is currently being applied to your text.

6.2 Styles in a blank document

Each document you create in Word will have several styles already set up. You can view the styles available in the Styles Formatting Task Pane or the Style List.

To display the styles available in your current document:

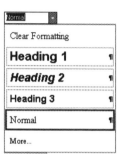

- Click the drop-down arrow to the right of the **Style** box to display the Style List.

Or

- Click [icon] or **More…** at the bottom of the Style List to display the **Styles and Formatting** Task Pane.

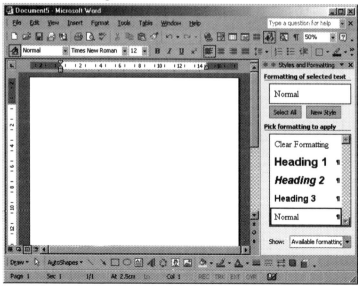

The styles listed are available to you each time you create a new blank document. They are stored in the Blank Document template.

You can either apply a style to text as you key the text in, or enter the text and then go back to select it and apply the style.

To apply a style to new text:

1 Select the style required from the Task Pane or Style List

2 Type in your text

3 Press [**Enter**]

To apply a style to existing text:

1 Select the text you want to apply a style to

2 Select the Style you require from the Task Pane or Style List

Blank document basic style options

Clear Formatting will remove all formatting and return the selected text to the Normal style.

Heading 1 Arial, size 16pt, bold, left aligned, spacing 12 pt before, 3 pt after

Heading 2 Arial, size 14pt, bold, italic, left aligned, spacing 12 pt before, 3 pt after

Heading 3 Arial, size 13pt, left aligned, spacing 12 pt before, 3 pt after

When you press [**Enter**] after the *Heading* styles, the paragraph style used for the following paragraph returns to *Normal* automatically.

Normal Times New Roman, size 10pt, spacing before and after 0 pt

More... displays the Styles and Formatting Task Pane.

Lots and lots of styles

Many styles are already set up in Word – far more than those displayed in the style list. Different styles are recorded in the various templates (patterns on which your documents are based), and are automatically available to you when you create a document using these templates.

You can however, display a list of all the styles from all the different templates if you wish. Choose **All Styles** from the **Show** field on the Task Pane, or hold down **[Shift]** and click the drop-down arrow to display the Style List. Once you've selected a style it will be added to the Style List in your document.

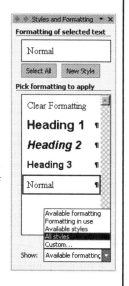

The **Show** list at the bottom of the Task Pane is used to display the Style and Formatting options you require.

Available formatting – displays the formatting options and Styles available to the current document.

Formatting in use – displays the formatting options actually in use in the current document.

Available Styles – displays the styles that are available (not manual formatting options specified) in the current document.

All styles – displays all the Styles available in Word.

Custom… – allows you to customize the list of format settings displayed under each of the above categories.

6.3 Creating a new style

If you want to use styles, but the formatting specified in the standard Word styles isn't what you want, you can create your own user-defined Styles, or modify the styles that are set up (see 6.4).

To create a new style:

1   Display the **Styles and Formatting** Task Pane (click 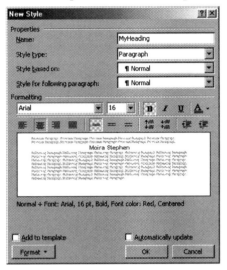)

2   Click the [New Style] button

3   Complete the **New Style** dialog box as required – give it a name and select the options from the drop-down lists

4   Use the formatting tools to format the style as required

•   To access all the formatting options, click the **Format** button and set the formats required from there

5   If you wish to add your style to the document template (so that it will be available to all other documents based on this template) select the **Add to template** checkbox

6   Select the **Automatically update** checkbox if you wish the style to be automatically updated anytime you apply manual formatting to text formatted with it within a document (all text within the document formatted with the style will be automatically updated too)

7   Click **OK**

Your style will appear on the Style List for the document (and will be available to all new documents using the document template if you chose the **Add to template** option).

You can also access the **New Style** dialog box from the **Format Settings** dialog box.

1 Choose **Custom...** from the **Show** list in the Task Pane
2 Click **Styles...** in the **Format Settings** dialog box
3 Click **New...** in the **Style** dialog box

6.4 Modify a style

If you have created a style, and selected the **Automatically update** option at the New Style dialog box, updating the style is easy. Simply change the formatting of any text that has the style applied to it. The style will update and any other text that has the style applied to it will by updated to reflect the changes.

*   If you have created a style without choosing the **Automatically update** option, a new formatting entry is listed in the Task Pane when you apply manual formatting to text that has the style applied to it e.g. Heading 1 + Red.

To modify a style that has not been set to Automatically update:

1 In the Styles and Formatting Task Pane, right-click on the style that you want to modify

2 Choose **Modify Style...**

3 Edit the style as required in the **Modify style** dialog box

4 Click **OK**

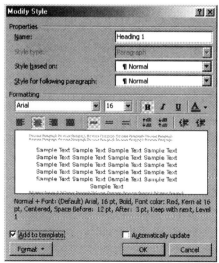

6.5 Style management

You can perform some Style management tasks – delete, re-name and copy – from the Organizer dialog box. You can also delete your own Styles from the Style and Formatting task pane. You can delete your own Styles, but not those that are pre-set in Word.

To delete a Style (from the task pane):

1 Right-click on the Style name in the Styles and Formatting Task Pane

2 Choose **Delete**

3 Respond to the prompt – click **Yes** to confirm the deletion, **No** if you've changed your mind

♦ If you delete a style, any text in your document that had that style applied to it will have the *Normal* style applied

Or

1 Open the **Tools** menu and choose **Templates and Add-Ins...**

2 Click **Organizer...**

3 Select the style you want to delete from the lists

4 Click **Delete**

5 Confirm the **deletion**

6 Close the **Organizer** dialog box

The Organizer Styles tab

It you have a document open when you go into the Organizer dialog box, the styles in the current document and those in the template on which that document is based will be listed on the Styles tab.

If you don't want to work with the files that are currently open, you can close either or both in the Organizer dialog box, and open the files required. When you close a file in the Organizer dialog box, the Close File button becomes the Open File button, and you can click this and go on to locate and open the file you want to use.

When you go to open a file from the Organizer dialog box, the default file type listed in the Open dialog box is Templates. If you want to open a document, change the **Files of type** field to Word documents.

To rename a style:

1 Open the **Tools** menu and choose **Templates and Add-Ins...**

2 Click **Organizer...**

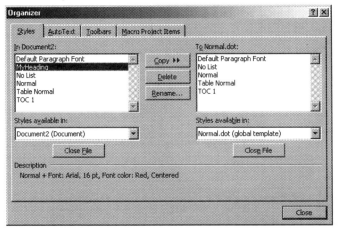

3 If necessary close the file displayed and open the file you require

4 Select the style you wish to rename

5 Click **Rename...**

6 Enter the new name

7 Click **OK**

8 Click **Close** to close the **Organizer** dialog box

You can copy styles from one file to another using the Organizer dialog box. If you have created some new styles in your document, then decide you should have stored them in the document template, you can quickly copy them over using this method.

To copy a style:

1 Open the **Tools** menu and choose **Templates and Add-Ins...**

2 Click **Organizer...**

3 Select the style you want to copy

4   Click **Copy**

5   Close the Organizer dialog box

6.6 Style Gallery

You can preview the styles from any template through the Style Gallery. If you wish, you can apply the styles from the template you preview to the current document.

1   Open the **Format** menu and choose **Theme...**

2   Click the **Style Gallery...** button

3   Select the template you want to preview the styles from

4   Do you want to preview the styles from the template using your current Document, an Example or Style samples? Select from the Preview options listed. The Preview window will display the styles from the template using the selected preview option.

5   If you want to apply the styles from the template to your current document, click **OK**, if not, click **Cancel**

•   If the style you want hasn't been installed, follow the instructions to install it.

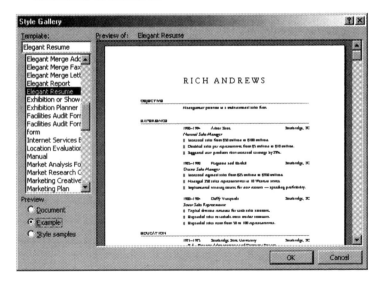

Has it changed?

If you have not used styles in your current document, and you opt to preview the styles using the Document option, there will be little or no change in the preview window.

However, if you have formatted your document using styles, and the template you select in the Style Gallery has styles of the same name but with different formatting, the changes to your document may be quite dramatic.

Summary

In this chapter we have discussed styles. Styles are important for a number of reasons – not least that they improve efficiency by increasing your speed, and ensuring consistency within and across your documents.

You have learnt how to:

◆ Use the in-built styles that come with Word.

◆ Create your own user-defined styles.

◆ Edit styles.

◆ Manage your styles by deleting, renaming and copying.

◆ View styles from different templates through the Style Gallery and apply them to your document.

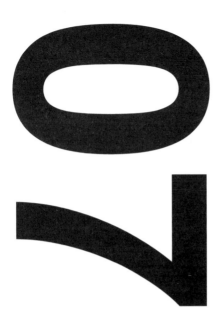

7
tables

In this chapter you will learn

- how to create tables
- how to manipulate tables
- how to sort the data in tables
- about calculations in tables
- how to create a chart from data in a table

Aims of this chapter

In this chapter you will find out just how useful and versatile tables can be for all kinds of things. Tables can be used when you need to enter text in a parallel column layout, or if you need to design forms. If your table contains numeric data, you can perform basic calculations on that data.

7.1 Table basics

Tables consist of rows and columns. Where a row and column intersect, we have a cell.

COLUMN

ROW

To create a table:

1 Place the insertion point where you want your table to go

2 Click the **Insert Table** tool on the Standard toolbar

3 Click and drag over the grid that appears until you get the number of rows and columns required

4 Release the mouse button – you have an empty table

If you have your non-printing characters displayed, you will notice markers at the end of each cell and row that look a bit like a sun! Click to hide the non-printing characters if they distract you.

You can move around your table using the keyboard or the mouse.

♦ Press the [**Tab**] key to move forward to the next cell.

♦ Press [**Shift**] and [**Tab**] to move back to the previous cell.

Or

♦ Click in the cell you want to move to.

To select a cell:

♦ Click just inside the left edge of the cell.

To select several cells:

♦ Click and drag over the cells you want to select.

Or

1 Click in the corner cell of the range of cells.

2 Point to the cell in the diagonally opposite corner.

3 Hold down [**Shift**] and click the left mouse button.

To select a column:

♦ Click the **top** gridline or border of the column you want to select (you should get a black arrow pointing downwards).

♦ To select adjacent columns, drag along the top border.

To select a row:

♦ Click to the **left** of the row you want to select.

♦ To select adjacent rows, drag up or down the row selector area.

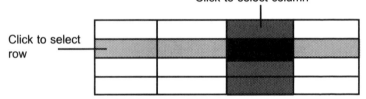

Click to select column

Click to select row

Other things to note:

♦ When you create your table, each column is the same width, and the table stretches across the page.

♦ To enter text or data, go to the cell – click in it or press [**Tab**] or [**Shift**]+[**Tab**] to reach it – then just type!

♦ Text will automatically wrap once it reaches the right edge of the cell, and the row will deepen to accommodate it.

♦ Text and numbers automatically align to the left of a cell.

♦ If you press [**Tab**] when the insertion point is in the last cell in the last row of your table, a new row is created.

♦ You can format your cells, or text within the cells, using the normal formatting commands.

7.2 Column width and row height

Column width

In most cases, you won't want all your columns to be the same width – it depends what you're entering into them. You can easily change the column width. There are several methods you might like to try out.

AutoFit

You must have some text or data in your columns to give AutoFit something to work on.

To adjust the column widths for all columns in the table:

1 Click anywhere inside the table

2 Open the **Table** menu and choose **Autofit…**

3 Click **AutoFit to Contents**

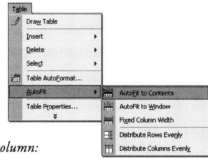

To adjust the width of a column:

◆ Double-click the border or gridline to the right of the column. The column width will adjust automatically to give a 'best fit' for that column.

Address	Notes	Cost
Old Mill Inn 24 Mill Lane Melrose	Delightful retreat in the Scottish borders. Food available from 10 am through until 10 pm. Excellent lunches and evening meals. Accommodation available. Working waterwheel, herb garden and riverside walks.	Lunches from £4 Dinner from £11.50 Dinner, Bed and Breakfast: £35 per head
Kathy's Kitchen 12 High Street Duns	Excellent family run coffee shop. Soup, baked potatoes, sandwiches, etc. available all day. Delicious home baking!	Various.

Manual adjustment

1 Position the mouse pointer over the border or gridline to the right of the column, below the top horizontal gridline of the table

2 Click and drag the border or gridline as required

Or

♦ Click and drag the **Move Table Column** marker (on the ruler) which is above the right border of the column.

Using the Table Properties dialog box:

1 Choose **Table Properties...** from the **Table** menu

2 On the **Column** tab, locate the column you want to adjust – use the **Previous column/Next column** buttons

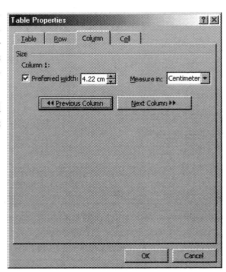

3 Set the **Preferred width** of column as required

4 Click **OK**

♦ Double-click on a **Move Table Column** marker to open the **Table Properties** dialog box.

Row height

Row height can also be adjusted. By default the row height adjusts automatically as you enter your text. If you wish to set a minimum row height, or an exact row height (perhaps for forms) you can do so in the Table Properties dialog box.

1 Select **Table Proper-
ties** from the **Table**
menu

2 Open the **Row** tab

3 If necessary, use the
Previous Row or
Next Row buttons
to locate the row
you want to adjust

4 Select the **Specify
height** checkbox if
necessary

5 Set the *Specify height*
and *Row height is*
options

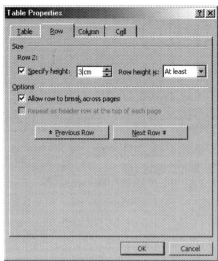

♦ **At Least** specifies a minimum row size. If you enter
enough text so that a deeper row is required, Word will
automatically adjust the height to accommodate it.

♦ **Exactly** sets a fixed row size. If you enter more text than
will fit in the row, Word will not adjust the row height.

6 Click **OK**

If you are in Print Layout view, **Adjust Table Row** markers are
displayed on the vertical ruler when the insertion point is inside a table. You can click and drag these to adjust the height
of a row. When you adjust a row height in this way it adopts
the **At least** height option.

7.3 Insert and delete rows, columns and cells

When working with your table, you may find that you need to
insert (or delete) rows or columns.

To insert a row:

1 Display the **Tables and Borders** toolbar – click the **Tables
and Borders** tool ![icon] on the Standard toolbar

2 Position the insertion point within the row that will be above
or below the row you are about to insert (if you want to add

more than one row, select the number of rows required – that number of new rows will be inserted)

3 Click the drop-down arrow to the right of the **Insert Table** tool on the Tables and Borders toolbar

4 Select the option required – *Insert Rows Above* or *Insert Rows Below*

* Note that the **Insert Table** tool changes to the tool that indicates the option selected from the list.

Or

* Select and right-click on the row(s), then click on **Insert Rows** (the row(s) will be inserted *above* the selected area).

Contact	Address	Notes	Cost
Jill Syme	Old Mill Inn 24 Mill Lane Melrose	Delightful retreat in the Scottish borders. Food available from 10 am through until 10 pm. Excellent lunches and evening meals. Accommodation available. Working waterwheel, herb garden and riverside walks.	Lunches from £4 Dinner from £11.50 Dinner, Bed and Breakfast: £35 per head
Kathy or Anna	Kathy's Kitchen 12 High Street Duns	Excellent family run coffee shop. Soup, baked potatoes, sandwiches, etc. available all day. Delicious home baking!	Various.

To insert a column within a table:

1 Select the column that will be to the right or left of the new column you are about to insert (if you want to add more than one column, select the number of columns required – that number of new columns will be inserted)

2 Click the drop-down arrow to the right of the **Table** tool on the Tables and Borders toolbar

3 Select the option required – *Insert Columns to the Left* or *Insert Columns to the Right*

Or

♦ Select and right-click on the column(s), then left-click on **Insert Columns** (the column(s) will be inserted to the **left** of the selected area).

♦ You may find that you have to adjust the width of your columns to accommodate the new columns you add.

To insert cells:

1 Select the area that you wish to insert cells into

2 Click the drop-down arrow to the right of the **Table** tool on the Tables and Borders toolbar

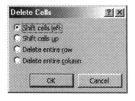

3 Choose **Insert Cells...**

4 Complete the dialog box as required

5 Click **OK**

To delete a row, column or cells:

1 Select the row (or rows), column (or columns) or cells that you want to delete

2 Right-click on the selected area then left-click on an option

Or

3 Open the **Table** menu and choose **Delete**

4 Select the option required

5 If you opt to delete cells, select the desired option from the dialog box and click **OK**

To delete an entire table:

1 Place the insertion point anywhere inside the table

2 Choose **Delete** from the **Table** menu

3 Select **Table**

If you press the [**Delete**] key, the *contents* of the table are deleted, but the table remains in place.

7.4 Merge and split cells

There will be times when you need to merge cells to achieve the effect you want within your table. For example, if you want to insert a heading that spans several columns you will need to merge several cells together in the heading row.

To merge cells:

1 Select the cells you want to merge

2 Click the **Merge Cells** tool 🖻 on the Tables and Borders toolbar

◆ The selected cells will combine to become one cell.

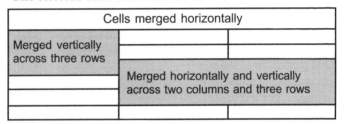

You may also find that you need to split cells to get the effect you require in your table. There are variations on a theme when it comes to splitting cells – I suggest you experiment with this one until you get the hang of how it works.

To split cells:

1 Select the cells you want to split

2 Click the **Split Cells** tool 🖩 on the Tables and Borders toolbar

3 Complete the dialog box as required

4 Click **OK**

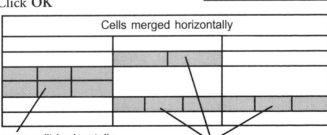

Deep row split horizontally and vertically

Split vertically

As you can see, you could design some pretty complicated forms by utilizing the merge and split cell features.

Re-sizing a table

If you create a table e.g. 3 columns by 6 rows, then discover you should have made it 4 columns by 6 rows, select the whole table, then use Split Cells and specify the number of columns and rows required. Leave the **Merge cells before split** checkbox selected and click **OK**.

7.5 Drawing tables

You may prefer to 'draw' your tables onto your page. You can draw your table and make rows and columns very easily in Word.

To draw a table:

1 Display the Tables and Borders toolbar – click the **Tables and Borders** tool ⊞ on the Standard toolbar if required

2 The **Draw Table** tool is automatically selected (if you had the Tables and Borders toolbar displayed already, click the **Draw Table** tool ✎ to select it)

3 Click and drag on your page to draw a rectangle the size you want your table to be

4 Draw in rows and columns where you want them

5 Switch the **Draw Table** tool off when you've finished – click ✎ or press [**Esc**]

To remove a line drawn in the wrong place.

1 Select the **Eraser** tool ⬚

2 Click and drag on the line you want to remove

3 Press [**Esc**] to cancel the **Eraser** tool, or click ⬚ again

If you want to have your rows or columns the same height or width, it can be a bit tricky when drawing a table in this way. You could use the **Cell** or **Row** tab in the **Table Properties** dialog box to help you even things up – or you could use the **Distribute Rows Evenly** or **Distribute Columns Evenly** tools.

To distribute the row height evenly:

1   Select the rows you want to equalize

2   Click the **Distribute Rows Evenly** tool ⊞

To distribute the column width evenly:

1   Select the columns you want to equalize

2   Click the **Distribute Columns Evenly** tool ⊞

All the normal table handling features can by used in a drawn table.

Tables and Borders toolbar

Experiment with the tools on the Tables and Borders toolbar to see what effect they have on your data. The toolbar gives you shortcuts to many of the options you will use when working with tables.

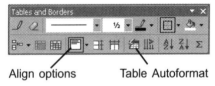

Align options   Table Autoformat

The table below has the text and data centred vertically and horizontally (**Align Center**) in each cell, and has the *Table Colorful 1* Autoformat applied to it. To apply an Autoformat, click **Table AutoFormat** on the toolbar or select **Table AutoFormat** from the **Table** menu and pick a format from the dialog box.

Book Sales (no of books) 1ˢᵗ Quarter 2003			
	January	February	March
Children's	500	650	543
Adult Fiction	450	430	654

7.6 Sorting data in tables

Tables are often used to produce a list of data – names and phone numbers, stock items, student names, etc. Lists often need to be manipulated and sorted into different orders – this is easily done in a table.

The table below could be sorted in a number of ways:

- On a single column, e.g. Country order or Town order
- An alphabetical listing on Surname then Firstname order
- A listing in Country, Town then Surname order

You can sort on up to 3 levels at a time.

Firstname	Surname	Address	Town	Country
Jill	Wilson	22 High St	Birmingham	England
Robert	Adamson	4a Mill Wynd	Greenlaw	Scotland
Malcolm	Simpson	Western Cottage	Perth	Scotland
Alison	Birch	10 High Croft	Birmingham	England
Carol	Adamson	Summerfield Way	Perth	Scotland
Rebecca	Jackson	102 Lower Lane	Cardiff	Wales
Gordon	Peterson	13 Grange Loan	Edinburgh	Scotland
Penny	Fullerton	82 All Saints Way	Cork	Ireland
James	Russell	2a Ferry Lane	Ascot	England

To perform a simple sort, on one column:

1 Place the insertion point in the column you want to sort

2 Click the **Sort Ascending** ![Sort Ascending icon] or the **Sort Descending** tool ![Sort Descending icon] on the Tables and Borders toolbar

- A simple sort assumes that the first row in your table is a header row (containing column labels) and it is not included in the sort.

To sort the list on Surname then Firstname order

1 Position the insertion point anywhere within the table

2 Open the **Table** menu and choose **Sort...**

3 Complete the dialog box as required – sort by *Surname*, then by *Firstname*

4 Click **OK**

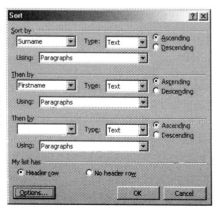

Note that:

♦ You can sort in ascending or descending order

♦ Different types of data can be sorted – Text, Number or Date – in an appropriate order for the type

♦ The table may or may not have a Header Row. The Header Row is the first row in your table – it usually contains column headings. If the first row is to be sorted along with the other rows, select the **No header row** button.

Firstname	Surname	Address	Town	Country
Carol	Adamson	Summerfield Way	Perth	Scotland
Robert	Adamson	4a Mill Wynd	Greenlaw	Scotland
Alison	Birch	10 High Croft	Birmingham	England
Penny	Fullerton	82 All Saints Way	Cork	Ireland
Rebecca	Jackson	102 Lower Lane	Cardiff	Wales
Gordon	Peterson	13 Grange Loan	Edinburgh	Scotland
James	Russell	2a Ferry Lane	Ascot	England
Malcolm	Simpson	West Wind Cottage	Perth	Scotland
Jill	Wilson	22 High Street	Birmingham	England

Table sorted by *Surname* then by *Firstname*

7.7 Simple sums

You can do some calculations in a table. If you use Excel as well as Word, it's often easier to insert a worksheet into your document (see section 14.3), and use Excel's functions. However, if you want to do calculations in Word, here's how!

Position the insertion point inside the cell you want to contain a formula.

1 Open the **Table** menu and choose **Formula...**

2 If the Formula suggested is not the one you want, delete it and enter the right formula

3 If you want to specify a number format, e.g. currency, select it from the **Number Format:** list

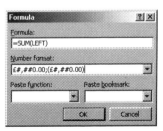

Sales Figures (in £s)				
	JAN	**FEB**	**MAR**	**TOTAL**
Bill	12,300	10,500	9,750	32,550
Ann	14,320	12,300	10,650	37,270
Bert	10,430	8,450	12,500	31,380
TOTAL	37,050	31,250	32,900	101,200

The formulae are entered as fields in your table.

• The AutoSum tool Σ on the Tables and Borders toolbar inserts the formula =**Sum** (**above**) or =**Sum** (**left**) in the cell that the insertion point is in.

If you change any of the figures that feed your formulae, the result *is not* updated automatically. Some of the figures have been changed in the table below, but the total row and column remain unchanged.

Sales Figures (in £s)				
	JAN	**FEB**	**MAR**	**TOTAL**
Bill	*19,300*	10,500	9,750	32,550
Ann	14,320	*22,300*	*19,650*	37,270
Bert	*50,430*	*18,450*	12,500	31,380
TOTAL	37,050	31,250	32,900	101,200

To update all the cells with formulae in them:

1 Select the entire table
2 Press [F9]

Sales Figures (in £s)				
	JAN	**FEB**	**MAR**	**TOTAL**
Bill	19,300	10,500	9,750	*39,550*
Ann	14,320	22,300	19,650	*56,270*
Bert	50,430	18,450	12,500	*81,380*
TOTAL	*84,050*	*51,250*	*41,900*	*177,200*

• The Formula fields are updated

- *To update a single field* – position the insertion point within it and press [**F9**].
- *To toggle the display of all the field codes in your document* – press [**Alt**]-[**F9**].
- *To toggle the display of a specific field code in your document* – place the insertion point in the field and press [**Shift**] + [**F9**].

The cells in the table are identified by cell addresses (or names) as they are in a spreadsheet. The first column is A, the second is B, etc. Rows are numbered 1, 2, 3, etc. A cell's address is derived from its row and column, e.g. A6, B7, D2. These addresses can be used in the formulae.

Acceptable formulae include:

=Sum (above)

=Sum (left)

=A7+B6

=A1-B2

=A3/B6

=A4*B4

=Sum (A1: A6)   The range of cells from A1 to A6

=Min (A3, A7, A11)   Three separate cells

=Count (B7: B14)   The range from B7 to B14

Check out **Formulas** in the on-line Help for more information.

7.8 Charting data

The data you enter into a table can be used to produce a chart. The first row and column of cells you intend to chart must have text in them, the other cells should contain numeric data.

1 Select the cells you want to create a chart from

Sales Figures (in £s)			
	JAN	FEB	MAR	TOTAL
Bill	19,300	10,500	9,750	39,550
Ann	14,320	22,300	19,650	56,270
Bert	50,430	18,450	12,500	81,380
TOTAL	84,050	51,250	41,900	177,200

2   Choose **Object** from the Insert menu

3   Select the **Create New** tab

4   Scroll through the list and choose **Microsoft Graph Chart**

5   Click **OK**

Your data is taken into the Graph Chart application, and you can work on it there. The default type is a Column chart. The column headings and row labels of the selected cells are used to label the x-axis and add a legend to explain the data.

You will notice that the Standard toolbar displays several tools to help you work with your chart. You can use the Charting tools or menu bar to manipulate your chart. Experiment with the various options to get the effect you want.

Some tips to get you started:

◆ Toggle the display of your datasheet using the **View Datasheet** tool.

◆ Use the **Chart Type** tool on the Charting toolbar to try a different style of chart.

◆ To edit an individual object on your chart, e.g. the legends, a column, the x-axis, etc., double-click on it and explore the dialog box that appears.

◆ To add a chart title, open the **Chart** menu and choose **Chart Options...** You can add titles on the Titles tab.

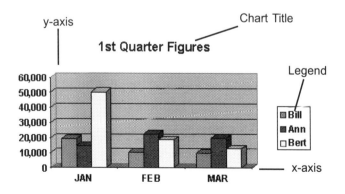

To leave Microsoft Graph Chart and return to your document:

• Click anywhere on your page, outside the chart area.

The chart becomes an *embedded* object (see section 14.1). It can be resized, moved or returned to Graph Chart for editing.

To resize the chart:

1 Select it – click on it once

2 Point to a handle in a corner or at the mid-edge of the object – the pointer becomes a double-headed arrow

3 Click and drag the handle to resize your chart

To move the chart:

1 Select it

2 With the mouse pointer anywhere within the chart object, drag and drop (or cut and paste) to reposition the chart

To return the chart to Microsoft Graph Chart:

• Double-click on the chart

To delete a chart:

• Select it and press [**Delete**]

Summary

This chapter has introduced tables – a very powerful and flexible feature in Word. We have discussed:

• Creating a table using the Insert Table method.

• Entering text and data into a table.

• Selection techniques within a table.

• Changing column widths and row heights.

• Editing the table structure by adding and deleting rows and columns, merging and splitting cells.

• Creating a table using the Draw method.

• Sorting data in tables.

• Simple calculations within tables.

• Charting data from a table.

08

multi-page documents

In this chapter you will learn

- about page breaks, headers and footers, and bookmarks
- how to use find and replace
- about footnotes and captions
- how to use the document map
- about outline and master document view
- how to create a table of contents and an index

Aims of this chapter

In this chapter we will consider some features that are useful when working with multi-page documents. Page breaks, moving through a long document, bookmarks, page numbering, headers and footers, footnotes, endnotes, captions and cross-references will be discussed. You will be introduced to Web Layout, Outline and Master Document view and learn how to create a table of contents and an index.

8.1 Controlling page breaks

Automatic page breaks

These are inserted when the text reaches the end of a page. You can set the options in the Format Paragraph dialog box:

1 Open the **Format** menu and choose **Paragraph**

2 Select the **Line and Page Breaks** tab

3 Select the **Pagination** options as required

* **Widow/Orphan control** prevents Word from printing the last line of a paragraph at the top of a page (widow), or the first line of a paragraph at the bottom of a page (orphan).

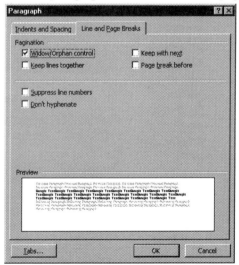

- **Keep lines together** prevents a page break within a paragraph.
- **Keep with next** prevents a page break between the selected paragraph and the following one.
- **Page break before** inserts a manual page break before the selected paragraph.

4 Click **OK**

In Normal view a dotted line appears across your screen when an automatic page break occurs.

In Print Layout view, the insertion point moves to the top of the next page when an automatic page break occurs.

Manual page breaks

If you need to, you can force a page break before you fill a page with text, rather than wait for automatic pagination to occur.

To insert a manual page break:

- Hold down the [**Ctrl**] key and press [**Enter**].

If you are in Normal view a dotted line will appear across your screen with the text **Page Break** in the middle of it.

Page Break

If you are in Print Layout view, the insertion point moves to the top of the next page.

- To remove a manual page break use [**Delete**] (if the page break is to the right of the insertion point) or [**Backspace**] (if the break is to the left of the insertion point).

8.2 Headers and footers

In multi-page documents 'headers' and 'footers' are often used for things like page numbers (imagine dropping a pile of unnumbered pages!). The header and footer areas are within the top and bottom margins. You can choose to have the headers and footers:

- The same on every page (this is the default option).
- Different for the first page of your document.
- Different on odd and even pages.

To create a header and/or footer:

1 Open the **View** menu and choose **Header and Footer**. The Header and Footer toolbar appears automatically – move it if necessary

2 Type your header

3 Click the **Switch Between Header and Footer** tool 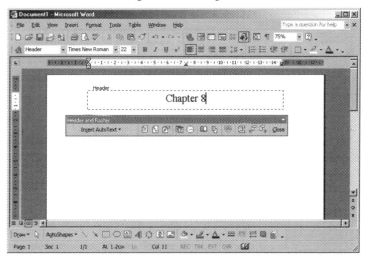 on the Header and Footer toolbar to move to the footer area and enter your footer text

4 Click the **Close** button on the toolbar when you've finished

Notice that there are two tabs set in the Header and Footer areas – a centre tab in the middle of the line, and a right tab at the right margin. Tab into these if you want to centre your header or footer, or align it to the right.

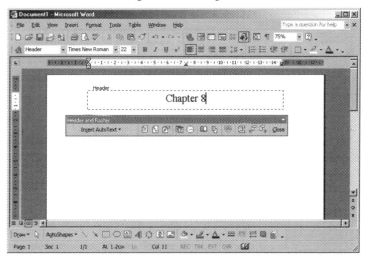

The Header and Footer toolbar contains useful tools for entering AutoText entries, page numbers, date, time, etc. and for changing your header and footer options.

Page numbers

DO NOT type a number in the header or footer area to insert a page number – you will get whatever number you type repeated on every page! Use the tools on the Header and Footer toolbar, or an AutoText entry, to create a page numbering field.

If you want to format the page number, or start numbering at other than 1, click the **Format Page Number** tool 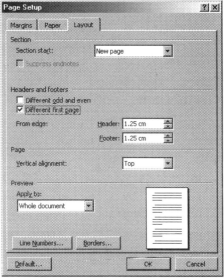 and format as necessary.

If you want the header or footer on your first page to be different to those on the other pages in the document (or you do not want it on the first page), go into the **Page Setup** dialog box.

1 Open the **View** menu and choose **Header and Footer**

2 Click the **Page Setup** tool

3 Select the **Different first page** checkbox on the **Layout** tab in the **Page Setup** dialog box

4 Click **OK**

5 Use the **Show Previous** and **Show Next** tools to move between your first page header or footer area, and the header or footer area for the rest of the document.

6 Enter your header and footer details as required

7 Click **Close** on the Header and Footer toolbar

Page Setup dialog box showing the Layout tab with Section, Headers and footers (Different first page checked), Page, and Preview sections.

Setting up a different header and footer for odd and even pages is done in a very similar way. Follow the same steps, but at **3** select the **Different odd and even** checkbox on the **Layout** tab.

• You can select both the **Different first page** *and* the **Different odd and even** checkboxes if you wish.

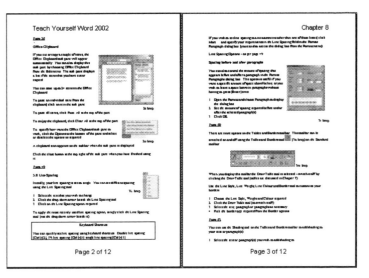

Edit a header or footer

You can easily edit a header or footer. Choose **Header and Footer** from the **View** menu (or double-click on the header or footer area of the page). Locate the header or footer and make the changes required.

Headers/footers and sections

If you want your header and/or footer to change part way through your document, you must insert a section break (see 4.1) at the place where you want them to change.

To create a different header or footer for part of your document:

1   Place the insertion point at the beginning of the text you want in your new section

2   Open the **View** menu and choose **Header and Footer**

3   Click the **Page Setup** tool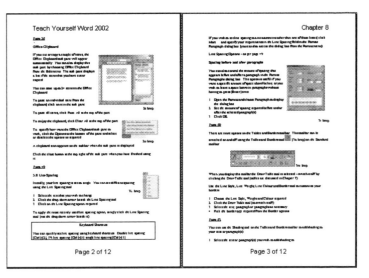

4   Select or deselect the options as necessary

5   In the **Apply to** field, select **This point forward**

6   Click **OK**

♦   Word inserts a section break at the end of the previous page and moves the insertion point on to the next page.

7 The Header area tells you which section you are in

8 By default the header or footer is the same as the previous one. To enter a different header or footer for this section click the **Same as Previous** tool ▦ to break the link, then enter the header or footer required

```
Header -Section 2-                    Same as Previous
```

Watermark

Watermarks are often used in long documents to display an image or text (e.g. Draft or Confidential) behind the text on each page. These watermarks can be created in Word using ClipArt or WordArt (see Chapter 11) and Headers and Footers.

To insert a watermark:

1 Open the **View** menu and choose **Header and Footer**

2 Insert the ClipArt or WordArt image required into the header or footer area

ClipArt

◆ Format the object so that the **Image Control** option (see *Formatting Pictures,* Chapter 11) is set to **Washout**, and the **Text wrap** option is **Behind Text**.

WordArt

◆ Set the text wrap option to **Behind Text**.

3 Move/resize the image to position it as required (anywhere on the page)

4 Click **Close** on the Header and Footer to return to your document

8.3 Moving through a long document

You probably use the scroll bars to move through your document most of the time. There are some other methods you might like to experiment with if you work with longer documents.

◆ Click and drag the scroll box on the vertical scrollbar – a prompt appears to tell you which page you're at. Release the mouse button when you reach the one required.

- To go to the top of the previous page click the **Previous Page** button at the bottom of the vertical scroll bar.

- To go to the top of the next page click the **Next Page** button at the bottom of the vertical scroll bar.

To go to a specific page number:

1 Double-click the page number indicator [Page 6] at the left end of the Status bar

2 Enter the page number you want to go to

3 Click **Go To**

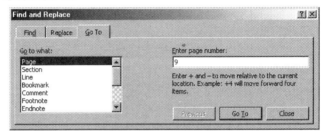

4 Click **Close**

- Experiment with the other options in the **Go to what:** list and use any that are useful to you.

Bookmarks

There may be times when you know that you will want to be able to return to a specific place in your file quickly. You should insert a 'bookmark' to mark the spot, then you can jump to the bookmark easily whenever you need to.

To insert a bookmark:

1 Place the insertion point or select the text or item you wish to mark

2 Open the **Insert** menu and choose **Bookmark**

3 Give your bookmark a name

4 Click **Add**

To jump to the bookmark:

1 Double-click the page number indicator at the left end of the status bar

2 Choose **Bookmark** from the **Go to what:** list

3 Select a bookmark from the **Enter bookmark name** list

4 Click **Go To**

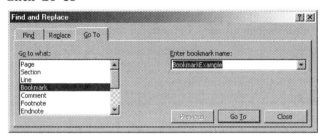

To delete a bookmark:

1 Open the **Insert** menu and choose **Bookmark**

2 Select the bookmark you want to delete

3 Click **Delete**

4 Close the **Bookmark** dialog box

Find and Replace

The Find and Replace commands can be useful when working with longer documents.

Find

The Find command allows you to locate specific text quickly. The Replace command enables you to find the specified text and replace it with other text – selectively or globally.

Find specified text:

1 Open the **Edit** menu and choose **Find…** (or press [**Ctrl**]-[**F**]) to display the **Find and Replace** dialog box

2 On the **Find** tab, enter the text that you are looking for

3 Click the **More…** button if you wish to display the options that you can specify for your text

4 Select the options as required

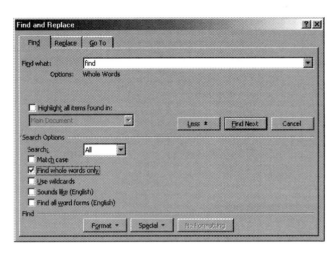

5 Use the **Format** button to specify any specific formatting that has been applied to your text

6 Click **Find Next**

7 Continue clicking **Find Next** until you have located the text

8 Click the **Cancel** button to close the dialog box and return to your document

You can use the Find command to quickly count the number of occurrences of a text entry in your document.

1 Complete the **Find** dialog box as required

2 Select the **Highlight all items found in** checkbox

3 Choose the area you want to search through from the list

4 Click **Find All**

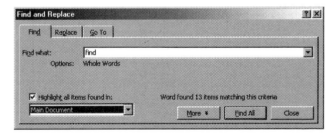

♦ Experiment with the options and use the dialog box Help button as necessary to explore this feature fully.

Find and Replace

Find and replace can be a very useful tool – especially if you've spelt a name wrong throughout a document!

1 Open the **Find and Replace** dialog box ([**Ctrl**]-[**F**])
2 Select the **Replace** tab
3 Enter the text you want to find in the **Find what:** field
4 Specify any options and formatting as necessary
5 Enter the replacement text in the **Replace with:** field
6 Specify any options and formatting as necessary
7 Click **Find Next**

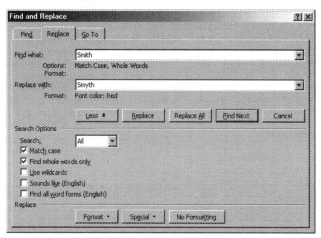

- ◆ Word will highlight the first occurrence of the text it finds.
8 Click **Replace** to replace this one occurrence, then click **Find Next** again

Or

- ◆ Click **Replace All** to replace all occurrences automatically.

8.4 Comments and Track Changes

When working on a document you can add *Comments* to the text.

You can also track your changes (insertions or deletions) so that you can then do a separate sweep to decide whether or not you actually want the changes accepted.

The features can be used at any time, but they are particularly useful when several people are working on the same document – comments can be added and amendments can be suggested, then a final decision can be taken on what to accept or reject.

The Reviewing toolbar has all the tools required for working with Comments and Tracked Changes.

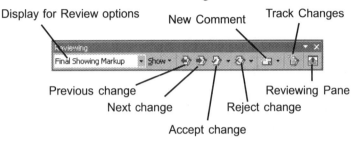

Display for Review options   New Comment   Track Changes

Previous change

Next change   Reject change

Accept change   Reviewing Pane

- **Display for Review** – specifies how Word displays changes and comments.

- **Show** – show or hide changes and/or comments.

Comments

To insert a comment:

1 Position insertion point

2 Click the **New Comment** tool or choose **Comment** from the **Insert** menu

3 Type in your comment

4 Press [**Esc**] or click anywhere in your document to continue

- Comments are displayed down the right of your page.

To edit a comment:

- Click inside the comment box and edit as normal.

Or

- Click the **Reviewing Pane** tool to display it and edit the text there. Click the Reviewing Pane tool again to close it.

To delete a comment:

1 Right-click on the comment

2 Choose **Delete Comment** from the menu displayed

To delete all comments:

- Choose **Delete All Comments in Document** from the options in the Reject Change/Delete Comment list.

- You can move quickly from one comment to the next using the Next and Previous tools on the Reviewing toolbar.

Track Changes

To switch the Track Changes option on and off:

- Click the **Track Changes** tool on the Reviewing toolbar or open the **Tools** menu and choose **Track Changes**.

To set options for tracking changes:

1 Click the **Show** tool and choose **Options**

2 Complete the dialog box as required

3 Click **OK**

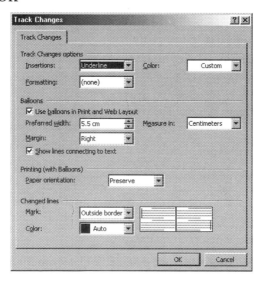

To accept/reject changes:

1 Click the **Next** (or **Previous**) tool on the Reviewing toolbar to move to a change (it may be easiest to work from the beginning of the document if you don't want to miss any)

2 Click the **Accept Change** or **Reject Change** tool (or choose from the list of options) as appropriate

8.5 Reference marks

Footnotes and endnotes

A footnote can be displayed below the text or at the bottom of the page. An endnote can be displayed at the end of the section or document. They are often used in longer documents to explain something mentioned in the main text – you've probably seen them in books or reports.

To create a footnote or endnote:

1 Place insertion point where you want the footnote/endnote marker to appear

2 Open the **Insert Menu** and choose **Reference**, **Footnote**

3 Select either **Footnotes** or **Endnotes** as required

4 Set the formatting options

5 Click **Insert**

6 Enter your footnote or endnote text

7 Click anywhere inside the main document area

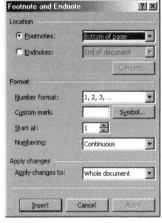

- The footnote/endnote text will be displayed when you move the mouse pointer over it. If it doesn't display, it is because the ScreenTips are turned off – **Tools**, **Options**, **View** tab, **ScreenTips** checkbox to switch ScreenTips on/off.

Edit/delete footnote/endnote

These can be edited and deleted like any other text.

- *To edit the note*, scroll to the end of the page or document and amend as necessary or double-click a footnote/endnote reference to go straight to the text.

- *To delete the note*, select the reference mark in the text and delete it. When you delete a mark, the associated footnote/endnote text is deleted. When you delete the note text the reference mark is *not* automatically deleted.

* *To change a footnote to an endnote,* select the footnote (text and number) at the bottom of the page, right-click on the selected area, and left click on **Convert to Endnote**.

Captions

A caption is another type of reference mark often used in longer documents. Captions can be added to tables, graphs, etc. and are displayed above or below the object.

To add a caption:

1 Select the object, e.g. table or graph

2 Open the **Insert** menu, choose **Reference** then **Caption...**

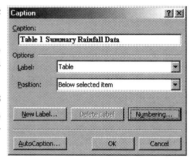

3 Complete the dialog box as required – edit the label, position, numbering format, etc.

4 Click **OK**

AutoCaptions

If you want to add captions automatically when objects are inserted, you can use the **AutoCaption** feature.

1 Click **AutoCaption...** in the **Caption** dialog box

2 Select the object you wish to add a caption to automatically

3 Specify the options required

4 Click **OK**

Each time you add a new object of the type specified a caption will be added.

Captions are displayed in text boxes (see section 11.4) and can be edited/deleted as such.

Cross-references

Cross-references can make it easy to jump from one place to another in a document. You cannot create a cross-reference to an object in another document. If you wish to do this you must combine them using a Master document (see 8.8).

To insert a cross-reference:

1 Type in the text to introduce the cross reference e.g. *'For more information, see ...'*

2 Open the **Insert** menu, choose **Reference**, then **Cross-reference**

3 Select the **Reference type:** from the list

4 Choose the **Insert reference to:** option required

5 Leave the **Insert as hyperlink** checkbox selected

6 Select the item to cross-reference to from the list

7 Click **Insert**

8 Close the **Cross-reference** dialog box

◆ To jump to a cross-reference in your document, hold down [**Ctrl**] and click on the cross-reference.

Browse by object

As you are discovering, a Word document can consist of many different *objects* – pages, bookmarks, footnotes, sections, comments, etc. You can browse through your document using these with the **Browse by Object** options.

To select the object you wish to browse by:

1 Click the **Browse by Object** button

2 Select the item from the options displayed

◆ Then use the Previous and Next buttons (above and below the Browse by Object button at the bottom of the vertical scroll bar) to move through your document.

8.6 Document Map

The Document Map can be displayed in any view – click the **Document Map** tool 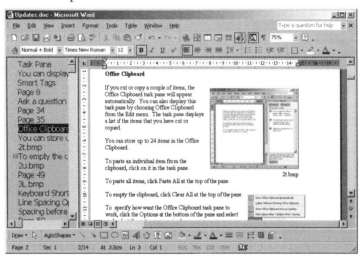 on the Standard toolbar to toggle it on and off.

You can use the Document Map to move quickly from one part of your document to another. You must have headings for the map to be useful (no headings results in an empty map). Simply click on the heading you want to move to.

Dragging its right-most edge can resize the Document Map pane – a Resize prompt appears when the mouse pointer is in the correct place.

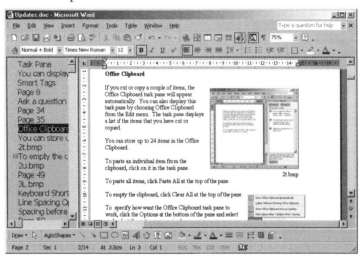

Your document is displayed at the right side of the screen, and the Document Map, displaying the outline structure of your document, is displayed down the left side of the screen. You can work on your document as usual in the main window.

8.7 Outline view

If you create long, structured documents – reports, minutes, theses, etc. – Outline view is worth experimenting with. It gives you an overview of the structure of your document by display-ing main headings, subheadings, etc.

It is often a good idea to go into Outline view and type in the structure of your document, then return to Normal or Print Layout view to enter the bulk of your text.

Alternatively, enter your text in Normal or Print Layout view, using the Heading 1 to Heading 9 styles to format the headings in your document. Word uses these styles to determine its structure when you take it into Outline view. Heading 1 is the highest level of heading you can have, Heading 9 is the lowest one. For most documents you'll probably use no more than four heading levels. Change to Outline view when you want view or edit the structure of your file.

Setting up the structure in Outline view

1 Create a new document

2 Click the **Outline View** tool ▤ (bottom left of the screen)

3 Type in the headings and sub-headings for your document – they are automatically formatted using the Heading 1 style

Outline view has its own toolbar to help you work on the structure of your document.

Demote ⬛ and promote ⬛ the headings to get the structure required, or use [Level 2 ▾], the level list.

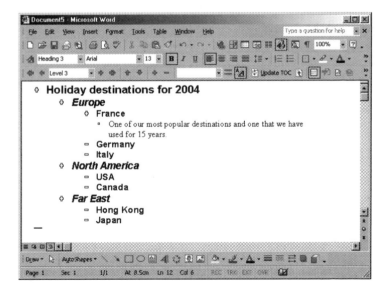

If you want to type in some body text (not a heading, but text formatted using the Normal style) in Outline view, click the **Demote to Body Text** tool ➡ then enter your text.

Notice ⊕ and ⊡ signs beside the headings. ⊕ means that the heading has sub-headings or body text under it, ⊡ means that there is nothing at a lower level. Body text has a ▫ to its left.

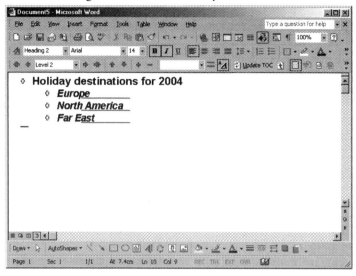

Collapse and expand

There may be times when you don't want to display the entire document in Outline view. You might want to view only the Heading 1 level paragraphs or your headings from level 1 to 2 only. In Outline view you can collapse or expand your documents to show just the level of detail required.

To collapse the whole document to a given level:

◆ Select the level from the **Show Level** list [Show Level 2 ▼].

To expand the whole document again:

◆ Select **Show All Levels** from the list.

To collapse or expand individual areas in your document:

1 Place the insertion point inside the heading of the area that you want to expand or collapse

2 Click the **Expand** ⊞ or **Collapse** ⊟ tool as required

To display only the first line of paragraphs at the body text level

- Click the **Show First Line Only** tool.

You can rearrange the structure of your document by moving large chunks of text very quickly in Outline view – much quicker than a cut and paste manoeuvre would allow.

To rearrange the structure of your document:

1. Collapse or expand your outline until you can see the heading you want to move – if you also want to move its sub-structure, collapse it, so you can just see the heading
2. Select the heading – place the insertion point within it
3. Click the **Move Up** or **Move Down** tool until the paragraph is in its new position

Any sub-structure the heading has will be moved with it.

Outline Levels

The Word styles Heading 1 – Heading 9 are assigned the outline levels 1 – 9 initially. You can assign you own styles to the outline levels. One way to do this is to base your styles on the Heading styles (they will automatically pick up the corresponding outline level when you do this). You can also format your styles to pick up the required outline level using the **Format**, **Paragraph** dialog box.

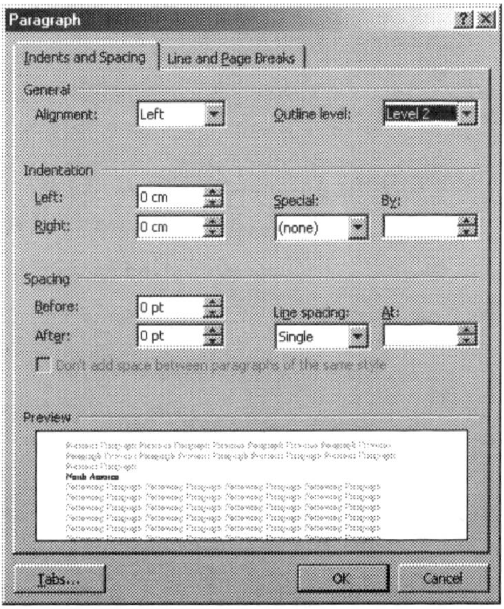

To assign you own Styles to the levels:

1 Display the **Styles and Formatting** Task Pane

2 Right-click on your style, then choose **Modify...**

3 Click the **Format** button and choose **Paragraph...**

4 Select the **Indents & Spacing** tab

5 Set the Outline level required in the **Outline level** field

6 Click **OK**

♦ You can also quickly assign levels to your text using the Level field on the Outlining toolbar.

8.8 Master Document view

A Master document is a container for other documents. It is a useful option for very long documents – long manuals or books – where you may have several files (perhaps one for each section of a manual, or chapter of a book) making up your final document.

By collecting the files together into a Master document, page numbering, headers and footers, table of contents and indexes can be generated more easily across all the subdocuments.

When you collect your subdocuments into a Master document, you have quick and easy access to each one without having to continually open and close individual files. You can either:

♦ Create subdocuments from within the Master document.

Or

♦ Insert existing documents into your Master document.

Go into Outline view to work with a Master document. The tools to the right of the Outlining toolbar are used to work with Master documents.

To create your subdocuments within your Master document:

1 Create a new file to be your Master document

2 Go into Outline view

3 Key in an Outline for your document (see section 8.7)

4 Select the headings and text you want to separate into sub-documents

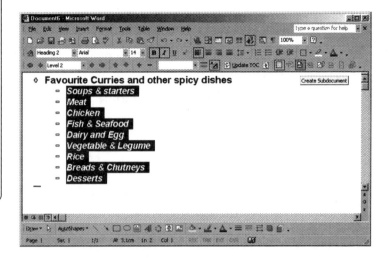

- Ensure that the first heading you select is formatted with the style you want to use for each subdocument. For example, if the heading for each subdocument is formatted using Heading 2, make sure that this is the level of the first text in the selection. Word will then create a new sub-document each time it finds a Heading 2 style.

5 Click the **Create Subdocument** tool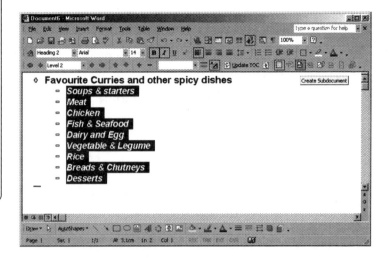

6 Save your Master document

- Word will automatically save each subdocument, with the subdocuments heading used for the file names.

- Word automatically inserts a continuous section break above and below each sub-document when you create them in this way. Click the **Master Document View** tool on the Outlining toolbar to toggle the display of the section breaks and Master Document tools.

To insert existing documents into your master document:

1 Display your Master document in Outline view

2 Place the insertion point where you want the document to go

3 Click the **Insert Subdocument** tool on the Outlining toolbar

4 Locate the file you want to insert

5 Click **Open**

- Word inserts a next page section break above and a continuous section break below the inserted document.

- When you insert a document into the Master document, the Master document must be expanded.

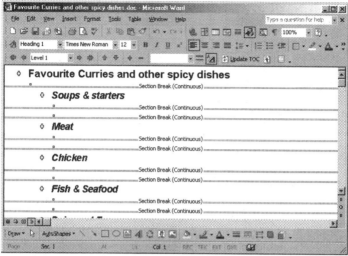

Master document showing section breaks

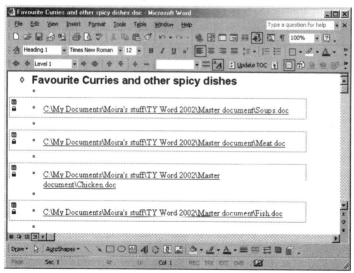

Master document after the subdocuments have been collapsed

When you Open a Master document the subdocuments are collapsed. Click the **Expand Subdocuments** tool 🔲 to expand them.

To open your subdocuments from the Master document:

• If the subdocuments are collapsed, press [**Ctrl**] and click on the name of the subdocument, or double-click on the subdocument icon to the left of the heading.

• If the subdocuments are expanded, double-click on the subdocument icon to the left of the subdocument heading.

When the subdocuments are expanded, you can use the Outlining toolbar to control the amount of detail displayed in your Master document (see *Collapse and Expand* in section 8.7).

Remove subdocument status

You can remove subdocument status from a document in your Master File. The text of the subdocument is converted to normal text within the Master File.

1 Expand your subdocuments

2 Select the subdocument you want to remove subdocument status from

3 Click the **Remove Subdocument** tool

To split an existing subdocument into more than one subdocument:

1 Expand your subdocuments

2 Enter a heading at the correct level at each point you want the document split

3 Select the original subdocument

4 Click the **Split Subdocument** tool

5 Save the Master document

A number of subdocuments can be merged into one:

1 Expand the subdocuments

2 If necessary, move the subdocuments you wish to merge so that they are next to each other

3 Select the documents – click the subdocument icon to the left of the heading of the first subdocument, then hold the

[**Shift**] key down and click the heading icon to the left of the last subdocument you want to merge

4 Click the **Merge Subdocument** tool

5 Save the Master document

Lock/Unlock subdocuments

All subdocuments are automatically locked when a Master document is collapsed. Locked documents cannot be edited from the Master document (but they can be opened from the Master document, edited and saved as usual).

When expanded, subdocuments are automatically unlocked. Unlocked documents can be edited from the Master document.

You can lock/unlock subdocuments that are expanded:

1 Select the document you wish to lock/unlock

2 Click the **Lock Document** tool

If you lock a document that is expanded in the Master document, you cannot edit it – it opens as a Read-Only file.

Unlock the subdocument again if you wish to edit it.

To print your Master document:

1 Expand the subdocuments in Master Document view

2 Go into Preview

3 Print as usual

8.9 Table of contents (TOC)

You can create a table of contents for any document very quickly, provided that you have used the built-in heading styles to format the headings (section 6.2), or you have assigned outline levels to the styles that you have used for headings (8.7).

1 Position the insertion point where you want your Table of Contents – usually at the beginning of your document.

2 Open the **Insert** menu and choose **Reference**, then **Index and Tables** (if you are in a Master document, and the subdocuments are not open, open the subdocuments when prompted).

3 On the **Table of Contents** tab select the number of **Show levels** and **Tab leader** if required

♦ If you wish to specify the styles that you want to use for your TOC entries click **Options** and specify them there.

♦ If you want to edit the formatting of the TOC entry, click the **Modify** button and edit the TOC styles as required.

4 Click **OK**

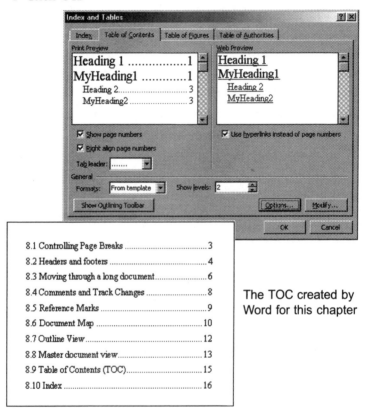

The TOC created by Word for this chapter

You can still get Word to generate a table of contents automatically, even if you haven't formatted your entries using the Heading 1– 9 styles.

You must enter *TC field codes* into your document to indicate where your table of contents entries are taken from. Then you generate your table of contents using these field codes.

1 Position the insertion point immediately in front of the text you are generating a TC code for

2 Open the **Insert** menu and choose **Field...**

3 Choose **Index and Tables** in the **Categories** list

4 Select **TC** in the field name list

5 Type the text you want to appear in the table of contents in the **Text Entry** area

6 Set the options as required and click **OK**

◆ TOC field codes are formatted as hidden text – click the **Show/Hide** tool on the Standard toolbar to display the code.

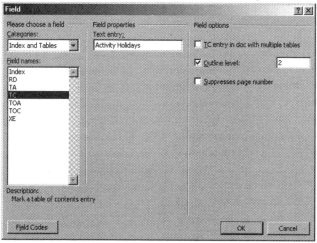

To generate a table of contents using Field Codes:

1 Place the insertion point where you want the table

2 Open the **Insert** menu and choose **Reference**, then **Index and Tables**

3 Select the **Table of Contents** tab

4 Click **Options...**

5 If you are not using heading styles, deselect the **Styles** checkbox

6 Select the **Table entry fields** checkbox

7 Click **OK**

♦ To quickly get to a page in your document, hold down [**Ctrl**] and click the TOC entry on your Table of Contents page.

♦ The Outlining toolbar has tools that will update and go to your TOC quickly.

8.10 Index

If your document needs an index, you can get Word to automate this process too. There are two steps to generating an index:

♦ Marking the entries you want to appear in the index.

♦ Creating the index.

To mark an index entry:

1 Select the word(s) you want to appear in your index

2 Open the **Insert** menu and choose **Reference**, then **Index and Tables**

3 Select the **Index** tab

4 Click **Mark Entry...**

5 The **Main entry** field will have the selected text – edit it if necessary

6 Click **Mark,** or **Mark All** if you want to index all the occurrences of the same text

7 The **Mark Index Entry** dialog box remains open so you can work through the document marking multiple entries

8 Click **Close** when you've finished

To create the index:

1 Place the insertion point where you want the index to appear – usually at the end of your file

2 Open the **Insert** menu and choose **Reference**, then **Index and Tables**

3 Select the **Index** tab

4 Specify the options required for your index

5 Click **OK**

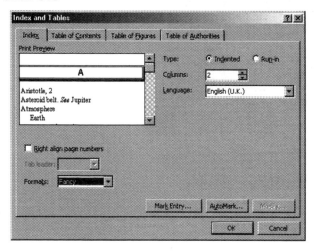

Summary

In this chapter we have discussed features that are particularly useful when you work with long documents:

• Automatic and manual page breaks.

• Headers and footers

• Page numbering.

• Moving through multi-page documents.

• Bookmarks and Find and Replace.

• Comments and Track Changes.

• Reference Marks.

• Document Map.

• Outline view and Master documents.

• Creating a table of contents and an index.

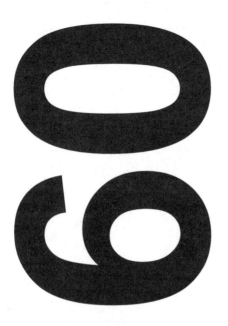

09

templates

In this chapter you will learn

- how to use the standard templates
- about customizing templates
- how to create templates
- how to build on-line forms
- ways of printing form data

Aims of this chapter

This chapter discusses templates – the patterns on which all your documents are based. So far, we have used the Blank Document template for most of our documents, and have had a look at some of the document wizards available (which are a bit like interactive templates) in Chapter 5. In this chapter, we will look at some of the other templates that come with Word, set up templates from scratch and design an on-line form.

9.1 Word templates

To create new documents using the Blank Document template you simply click the **New** tool on the Standard toolbar. The document has an A4 paper size, 2.54cm (1") top and bottom margin, 3.17cm (1.25") left and right margin and single line spacing. Paragraph and character styles that are part of the Blank Document template are available in the Style list on the Formatting toolbar, and the Styles and Formatting Task Pane.

Word comes with several other templates. Look through these as you may find some of them useful. There are several letter, memo, fax, and résumé (CV) templates to choose from. If you find a template you would like to use, you can customize it with your own company details, etc. and save it for future use.

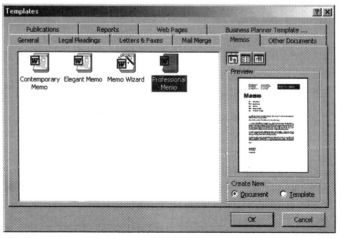

To create a document using a Word template (other than the Blank Document template):

1 Open the **File** menu and choose **New**

2 Choose **General Templates...** from the Task Pane

3 Select a tab to display the templates in each category (the *Blank Document* template is on the **General** tab)

4 Choose a template (not a wizard – see Chapter 5)

5 Click **OK**

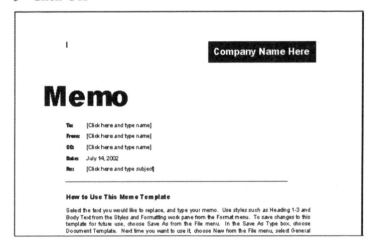

Explore the document that you have created. Check out the layout – notice that some templates, e.g. memo and fax, include areas for your company name, address, telephone/fax number, etc.

Many of the documents created using a Word template include details on how to use and complete the document. In the main, you just follow the instructions on the screen. Select and replace pieces of text that prompt you for your own details, e.g. **Company Name Here**. With other prompts, e.g. [**Click here and type name**], just do as you're told. The area is actually a Text Form Field – you'll learn how to set these up later (see section 9.3).

Check out the styles available in your document. You can edit these styles, or add to them (see Chapter 6 for more on styles).

9.2 Customizing the Word templates

If you find a template that you like to use, you can customize it with your own company details, name, address, etc. and save it for future use. If you don't customize it, you will need to enter the standard information on every document that you create using the original template. By customizing it, your own information will appear automatically on each new document.

You can customize any part of a template – not just the company detail areas. Page layout, headers, footers, styles, etc. can all be modified to suit your requirements.

To customize your template:

1 Create a new document using the chosen template

2 Customize it as required – enter your company details

3 Open the **File** menu and choose **Save As...**

4 In the **Save as type** field, choose **Document Template**

5 Select the folder in which you wish to store your template – either the *Templates* folder or one of its sub-folders

6 Give your template a name

• To replace the original template, save it in the same folder as the original and use the original template name.

• To keep the original template, save it with a different name.

7 Click **Save**

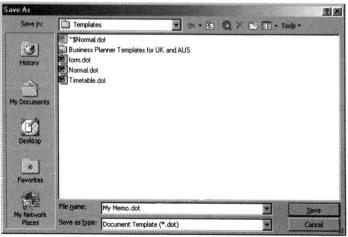

9.3 Creating your own templates

You can easily create your own templates to look like the letters, memos, faxes and forms you currently use.

To create your own template:

1 Open the **File** menu and choose **New**

2 Select **General Templates...** from the Task Pane

3 Choose the template to base your new template on – probably the *Blank Document* template on the **General** tab

4 Select **Template** from the **Create New** options

5 Click **OK**

A new template – with its temporary filename *Template1* displayed in the title bar – is created. Design your template – set margins, line spacing, add or edit styles, enter standard text, etc. – just as in a document file. Try designing a simple memo form similar to this example.

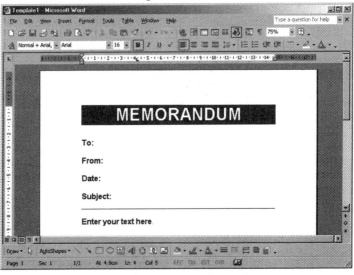

Form fields

To make your template easier to use, you can add special form fields to it. The **To:**, **From:** and **Subject:** prompts could be followed by Text form fields – so you can just click in them and key in the details. You could also add a Text form field to automatically display the current date after the **Date:** prompt.

The Forms toolbar is used to add fields to your file.

To display the Forms toolbar:

1 Point to any toolbar that is displayed and click the right mouse button

2 Left-click on **Forms**

Or

1 Open the **View** menu and choose **Toolbars**

2 Left-click on the **Forms** toolbar

You can hide or show any toolbar at anytime using either of the above techniques – the commands toggle the display of the toolbars on and off. (For more information on toolbars see Chapter 13.)

The Forms toolbar can be 'docked' to the right, left, top or bottom of the screen – drag and drop its Title Bar to position the toolbar.

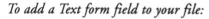

To add a Text form field to your file:

1 Place the insertion point where you want the form field

2 Click the **Text Form Field** tool

The form field will probably appear shaded – so you can see where it is. If it doesn't, click the **Form Field Shading** tool to switch the shading on.

To add prompts to the Text form fields:

• Double-click on the Text form field.

Or

1 Select the Text form field and click the **Options** tool

2 Enter the prompt in the **Default text:** field

3 Click **OK**

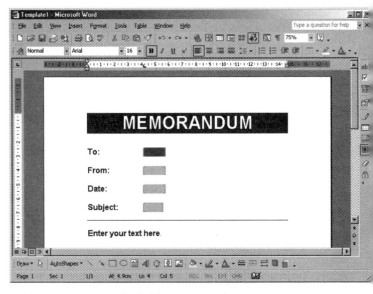

Add prompts to each field as required.

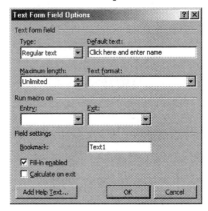

To get the date Text form field to complete automatically:

1 Create a Text form field after the **Date:** label
2 Double-click on the Text form field
3 Choose **Current date** from the **Type:** list
4 Select a format from the **Date format:** list
5 Click **OK**

Modify or complete your template as required, e.g. add page numbering to the page footer and then save your template.

To save your template:

1 Click the **Save** tool on the Standard toolbar

2 Select the folder you want to store your template in – the *Templates* folder or one of its subfolders.

◆ A template stored in the *Templates* folder will appear on the *General* tab in the **New** dialog box. If you want it on another tab, select the corresponding subfolder.

3 Edit the file name if necessary

4 Click **Save**

5 Close your template

◆ You can now create memos using your own template anytime your wish.

You can create templates for all the forms you use – order forms, invoices, booking forms, etc. Look through the Word templates to get some ideas. There are plenty of examples of many different layouts, including brochures, newsletters and directories.

9.4 Creating an on-line form

An on-line form is one that you complete using your computer. You can design on-line forms to look like the paper forms that you use, or adopt whatever layout you consider appropriate for your purposes.

For some forms, e.g. booking forms and invoices, it is often easier to design them using a table. You might also consider using other types of fields, e.g. checkboxes and drop-down lists.

This example introduces some other features that you can experiment with. The form was set up using a 2-column table, with cells merged in the title, booking confirmation and additional requirement rows.

Accommodation code, Description and *Booking Agent* fields are drop-down lists. The *Additional requirements* area contains a series of checkboxes.

Drop-down lists are useful when the data entered will be one item from a limited number of possible entries for the field.

To set up a Drop-Down form field:

1 Place the insertion point where the field should be

2 Click the **Drop-Down Form Field** tool

3 Double-click on the Drop-Down form field

4 Enter the text for the first item in the list in the **Drop-down item:** field

5 Click **Add**

6 Continue adding items to your list as required

• If you add an item in error, select it from the **Items in drop-down list** and click **Remove**.

• To move an item, select it in the list and click the up or down button.

7 Click **OK** when the list is complete

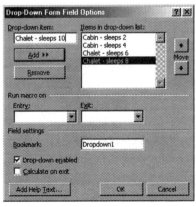

To set up a Check Box form field:

1 Place the insertion point where the field should be

2 Click the **Check Box Form Field** tool ☑

3 Add a prompt or caption

9.5 Protecting your on-line form

Once you've designed your form, you will want to prevent any-one changing it by accident, e.g. deleting form fields, chang-ing the standard text or the layout, etc. To safeguard your form, you should protect it. This has the following effects:

♦ Data entry and edit is limited to form fields – you can't change the template layout or standard information on it unless you unprotect your template again.

♦ Drop-down and Check Box form fields are activated.

You can protect your form quickly and easily using the Forms toolbar.

To protect your on-line form:

♦ Click the **Protect Form** tool 🔒 on the Forms toolbar.

This method of protecting a form is easy to use, but is not very secure, as all you have to do to unprotect the form is click the **Protect Form** tool. If you want more security you can assign a password to your form – then only those who know the pass-word can unprotect the form again.

Passwords can contain any combination of letters, numbers, spaces and symbols, up to 15 characters long.

To protect your form and give it a password:

1 Open the **Tools** menu and choose **Protect Document**

2 Select the **Forms:** option

3 Enter your password

4 Click **OK**

5 Re-enter the password at the prompt

6 Click **OK**

If your form consists of more than one section, the **Sections...** button will become active. If you don't want all of the sections protected, click the button and specify which should be protected.

Once you've completed your template, save it (in the Templates folder or one of its subfolders) and close it.

Careful with passwords

DO NOT forget your passwords – there is no magical way of unprotecting a form if you don't know the password!

Passwords are case-sensitive – you must enter the same pattern of upper and lower case characters each time you use the password.

9.6 Filling in your on-line form

Completing the form is very easy.

1 Choose **New** from the **File** menu

2 In the **New from Template** section of the Task Pane, click **General Templates...** or pick a recently used one from the list

3 Select your template, leave the **Create New** option at *Document* and click **OK**

4 Press the [**Tab**] key to move from one field to the next

5 Type in the details

• At a Drop-Down form field, click the drop-down arrow and select from the list.

• Click on a Check Box field to select it (click again to deselect it).

6 Save and print the document

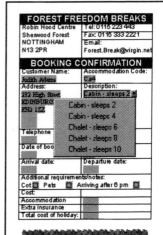

If you wish to print your on-line forms, you may have the choice of either printing onto plain paper, or onto a pre-printed form (if you've designed the on-line form to look like a paper form you currently use).

To print onto plain paper:

◆ Print in the normal way – the whole thing will print out – standard text, borders and data in the form fields.

To print onto pre-printed stationery:

1 Load the appropriate stationery into your printer

2 Choose **Print** from the **File** menu

3 Click the **Options...** button on the **Print** dialog box

4 Select the **Print data only for forms** checkbox

5 Click **OK** to close the dialog box and click **OK** to print

◆ Provided that the form has been protected, only the data entered into the form fields will be printed (no standard text, borders, etc. will be printed onto the form).

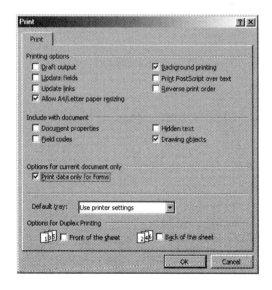

Summary

In this chapter we have discussed templates – those that come with Word and ones that you can create for yourself. You should know how to:

* Use the templates that come with Word.

* Customize the templates that come with Word.

* Create templates of your own.

* Create an on-line form.

* Protect an on-line form.

* Complete and print an on-line form on blank or pre-printed stationery.

mail merge

In this chapter you will learn

- how to set up a main document
- about data source files
- how to merge a main document with a data source
- about sorting and filtering
- how to create mailing labels and envelopes

Aims of this chapter

This chapter discusses mail merge. Mail merge is used to produce customized standard letters, forms or mailing labels. You will learn how to set up main documents, data documents and how to combine the two to produce your 'result documents'. Selective merge will also be addressed. With selective merge you combine only the data records that match specific criteria with your main document. You will also find out how to produce mailing labels.

10.1 Mail Merge terminology

Mail Merge uses jargon and techniques that are similar to those found in database applications. You are actually performing very basic database routines when you use mail merge.

* **Main document** – the document that contains the layout, standard text and field names that point to the data source.
* **Data source** – the file containing the records for the mail merge – perhaps a name and address file. The data source is usually in a table layout – it could be a Word file or an Access or Excel table. Other sources can be used – see the on-line Help for details. We will create ours in Word.
* **Record** – the information on each item in your data source.
* **Field** – a piece of data in a record. Title, surname, first name, telephone number, etc. would each be held in separate fields.
* **Field name** – the name used to identify a field.
* **Result document** – the document produced when you combine the records in the data source with the main document.

There are three steps involved in mail merge:

1 Creating the **main document**
2 Creating and/or locating the **data source**
3 Merging the two to produce the **result document**

It doesn't matter whether you create the main document or data source first – but you must have both to produce a result document.

10.2 Basic Mail Merge

If you are going to produce a Mail Merge letter, I suggest that you type and save the standard letter before you begin. If you wish to use an existing file, open the one that will be your main document. Then use the Mail Merge Wizard to step you through the process of setting things up.

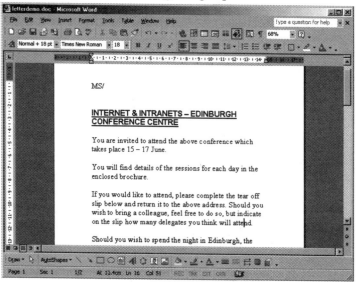

Create data document:

1 Open the **Tools** menu

2 Choose **Letters and Mailings**, then **Mail Merge Wizard**

3 The Mail Merge Task Pane will be displayed

4 At step 1 in the Wizard, choose *Letters* as your document type, then click **Next**

5 At step 2, choose *Use Current Document* – we are using the document that we have open, then click **Next**

6 At step 3, choose *Type a new list*, and then click **Create...** to set up the data source

7 Add details of your address list into the data file

8 Click **New Entry** when you have finished one record and want to enter another one

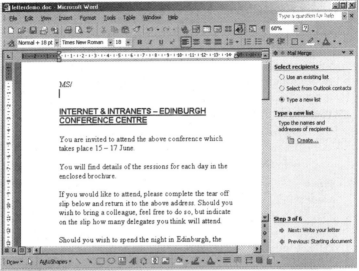

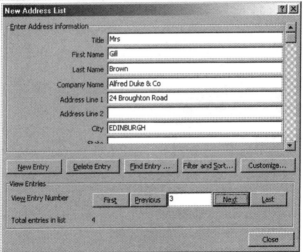

9 Click **Close** when you have finished

10 At the **Save Address List** dialog box, locate the folder that you want to save your data file to, name the file and save it

11 Click **Next** to move to the next step in the Wizard

• The Address List is saved as a Microsoft Access database.

Set up the main document:

1 At step 4, *Write your letter*, type in your letter (if necessary)

2 Place the insertion point where you want the address to go and click **Address Block** in the Task Pane

3 Set the options for your Address Block and click **OK**

4 Place the insertion point where you want the salutation and click **Greeting Line** – edit the set up as required and click **OK**

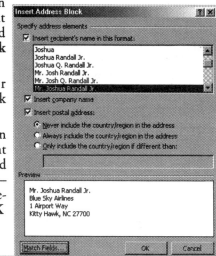

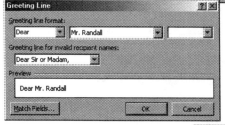

5 If you have any more fields to insert, position the insertion point as necessary and click **More Fields...**

6 Insert the fields required through the **Insert Merge Field** dialog box.

7 Close the dialog box when finished

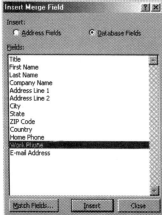

Produce the Result document

1 Click **Next: Preview your letters**, to see the results

2 At step 5, use the buttons near the top of the Task Pane to move through your letters and check the layout

3 If the layout is wrong, click **Previous** at the bottom of the Task Pane to return to step 4 and adjust the layout

4 Click **Next: Complete the merge** at the bottom of the Task Pane at step 5 to get to the final step

5 If all letters are fine, click **Print...** to print them out

6 If you wish to edit the letters, click **Edit individual letters...** to create a result document that you can edit and print.

7 Close the Task Pane when you've finished

10.3 Mail Merge toolbar

If you are already familiar with Mail Merge, or you prefer not to use the Wizard, you can use the Mail Merge toolbar. This toolbar appears automatically if you work through the Wizard. You can use the tools on this toolbar to work with your Mail Merge document.

The tools, from left to right

♦ **Main document setup**   Use to turn your document into a Mail Merge main document.

♦ **Open Data Source**   Opens your name and address list – usually an Access database or Outlook Contact list.

♦ **Mail Merge Recipients**   Sort and/or specify recipients from the data source.

♦ **Insert Address Block/Greeting Line/Merge Field**   Inserts field names that link the main document to the data source information.

♦ **Insert Word Field**   Helps you control how Word merges in data. See '*About mail merge field codes*' in the on-line Help.

♦ **View Merged Data**   Displays the results for the current record.

- **Highlight Merge Fields**   Shades the Merge fields.
- **Match Fields**   Lets you select the field name in your data source that corresponds to the information that Word expects.
- **Propagate Labels**   See 10.8.
- **First Record/Previous Record/Next Record/Last Record** Move through the records.
- **Find Entry**   Locates records where specified criteria are met.
- **Check for Errors**   Checks for errors in the field names or Word fields.
- **Merge to New Document/Merge to Printer/Merge to Email/Merge to Fax**   Destinations for the result document.

10.4 Editing the data source

The data source can be edited. New entries may be added, obsolete ones removed, or existing records can be edited.

1 Open the data source file (if necessary)
2 Click **Mail Merge Recipients**
3 Click **Edit…**

To add a record:

- Click **New Entry**.

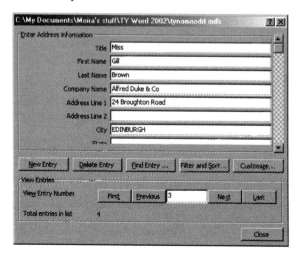

To delete a record:

1 Use the **First/Previous/Next/Last** buttons or **Find Entry...** to locate the record required

2 Click **Delete Entry**

To edit an entry:

1 Locate the record

2 Edit as required

3 Click **Close**

10.5 Sort and select recipients

By default, all the entries in your data source file will be merged with the main document. However, you can quickly sort the data source file, or select a subset of the records to merge.

1 Open the data source file (if necessary)

2 Click **Mail Recipients**

The selected records (those that will be merged) have a tick beside them.

- To select/deselect a record, tick or clear its checkbox.

- To select or deselect all entries, click **Select All** or **Clear All**.

- To select a group of records based on a set of criteria, e.g. all those who live in Edinburgh, click the arrow to the right of the field name and set the criteria (experiment with this!).

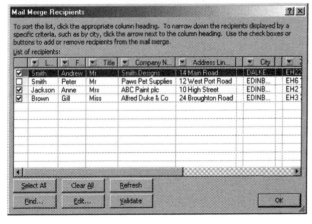

- To sort the entries, click the field name itself (at the top of each column). The sort order will alternate between ascending and descending each time you click.

A telephone list can be created quickly using the Directory document type.

TELEPHONE LIST		
Contact Name	Company	Telephone No
Paul Allan	Industrial Sciences & Chemicals Ltd	08687 1234
Johanne Andrews	Andrews Design Ltd	0141 445 5544
Jenny Gilmore	New Wave Designs plc	01692 44421
Steven Johnston	Swanson Electrical plc	01606 44312
William Jones	Happy Homes plc	012667 553399
Margaret McPherson	McPherson Foods	01904 555 121
Brenda Simpson	Good Food Ltd	08616 321
Peter Watson	PW Transport plc	01507 445 2211

10.6 Filter and Sort

To select groups of records based on more than one set of criteria, or perform a multi-level sort, you need to use the **Filter and Sort** dialog box.

Multi-level sort:

1 Open the data source file (if necessary)
2 Click **Mail Recipients**
3 Click **Edit...**
4 Click **Filter and Sort...**
5 On the **Sort Records** tab, set the sort order (up to 3 levels)
6 Click **OK**

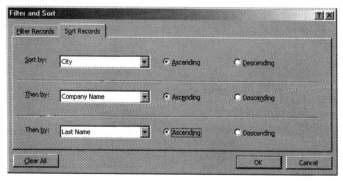

To filter by more than one set of criteria:

1 Open the **Filter and Sort...** dialog box

2 On the **Filter Records** tab, set up the selection rules (see below)

3 Click **OK**

Selection rules

- You can set up to six selection rules, joined by AND or OR.

- If all the selection rules must be met, link them with AND.

- If you want a record included using different selection rules, choose OR to separate each rule, or set of rules.

For example, to merge all records that contain 'Scotland' or 'England' in the *Country* field, you would need two selection rules linked by OR, e.g.

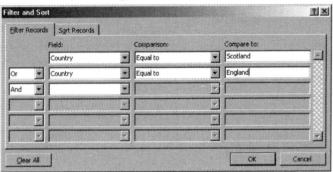

To merge all records that contain 'Scotland' in the *Country* field AND 'Perth' in the *City* field OR 'England' in the *Country* field, e.g.

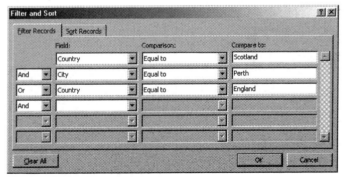

The next example will merge all records where the *Country* field contains 'Scotland' and also all records where the *Country* field contains 'England' *except* those records where the *City* field contains 'York'.

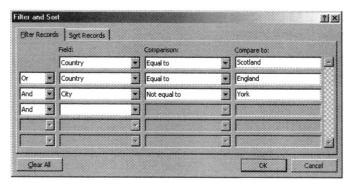

10.7 Edit the record structure

You can add, delete and rename fields in your data source file.

1 Open the data source file (if necessary)

2 Click **Mail Recipients**

3 Click **Edit…**

4 Click **Customize…**

To add a field name:

• Click **Add…** at the **Customize Address List** dialog box, complete the dialog box and click **OK**

To Delete a field name:

1 Select it in the **Field Names** list

2 Click **Delete**

To rename a field:

1 Select it in the **Field Names** list

2 Click **Rename**

3 Enter the new name

4 Click **OK**

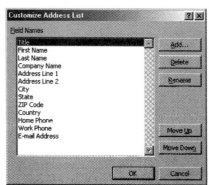

To reposition fields in the field list:

1 Select the field that you want to move

2 Click the **Move Up** or **Move Down** arrow as necessary

3 Click **OK** in the Customize Address List dialog box when you've finished

10.8 Mailing labels and envelopes

You can produce mailing labels or envelopes for your letters using the mail merge feature. The example here is for mailing labels – if you print onto envelopes, select **Envelopes...** at step 3 below – the dialog boxes that appear are very similar, only with options for envelope sizes rather than labels.

1 Create a new document – this will be the main document

2 Click **Main Document Set-up** on the Mail Merge toolbar

3 Choose **Labels** and click **OK**

You are taken into the **Label Options** dialog box so you can specify the label layout you will be using.

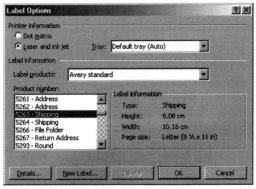

1 Edit the **Printer information** if necessary

2 Choose the **Label products** options

3 Select the **Product number**

♦ If you want further information on the label click **Details...**

♦ If you want to set up a custom label click **New Label...**

4 Click **OK**

- A table is created with columns and rows for each label.

5 Insert fields to lay out your first label

6 Click the **Propogate Labels** tool – this copies the label layout to each cell, with a **Next Record** field inserted

7 Merge to a **New Document** so that you can check the layout of your labels

8 If they look okay, save them if you wish, load up your label stationery and print the labels out.

I suggest you save the main document – then you don't need to create the label format again. In future you'll just need to:

1 Open the main document file for your labels

2 Open the data file that contains the names and addresses (using the **Mail Merge Helper** dialog box)

3 Merge and print out your labels

Miss Johanne Andrews Sales Manager Andrews Design Ltd Hilltop House 44 Hill Street GLASGOW Strathclyde G14	Mrs Brenda Simpson Office Manager Good Food Ltd Orchard House 24 Orchard Street GIFFORD Lothian EH39
Dr Paul Allan Development Manager Industrial Sciences & Chemicals Ltd 42 Dunbar Close HADDINGTON Lothian EH30	Mrs Margaret McPherson Director McPherson Foods 231 South View Road YORK Yorkshire
Mr Steven Johnston Support Technician Swanson Electrical plc 45 High Street WINSFORD Cheshire	Mr William Jones Property Consultant Happy Homes plc 44 York Lane MARTINSTOWN Co Antrim

Summary

This chapter introduced Mail Merge. We have discussed:

+ Setting up the main document.

+ Creating and editing a data source file in Word.

+ Merging the main document and data source file to create a result document.

+ Sorting the records to be merged into a specific order.

+ Filtering records so that you can include only records that meet the criteria required.

+ Editing the data source structure.

+ How to create and print mailing labels and envelopes.

pictures and drawing

In this chapter you will learn

- how to add impact with WordArt
- how to find and use Clip Art
- how to use the Drawing tools
- about picture fonts

Aims of this chapter

This chapter discusses some of the ways you can include text effects, pictures and drawings in your documents. We will consider how you can use WordArt, Clip Art, the Drawing toolbar and picture fonts to add impact to your documents.

11.1 WordArt

You can use WordArt to create eye-catching headings or text effects. You can access WordArt from the Drawing toolbar.

To display the Drawing toolbar:

♦ Click the **Drawing** tool on the Standard toolbar.

To insert a WordArt object into your document:

1 Place the insertion point where you want the object to go
2 Click the **Insert WordArt** tool on the Drawing toolbar
3 Select a style from the Gallery and click **OK**
4 Enter your text – edit the font as required – and click **OK**

The WordArt object appears in your document. It will be selected – with 'handles' in the corners and at the middle of each side. The WordArt toolbar will also be displayed.

♦ To de-select your WordArt object, click anywhere outside it. The WordArt toolbar will disappear when you deselect.
♦ To select the object again, click anywhere within it. The WordArt toolbar should appear again.

You can manipulate your WordArt object – resize, move, adjust or delete it – when it is selected.

To resize the object:

♦ Click and drag a square handle in the required direction.

To move the object:

♦ Move the mouse pointer inside the object – four arrows appear at the tip of the pointer – and drag and drop to move the object.

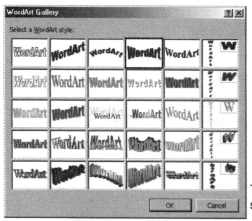

Pick a style

Type your text and set its font and size

Instant WordArt!

To adjust the object:

◆ Click and drag the adjust handle (displayed with most Text Wrapping options) as required.

To delete the object:

◆ Press [**Delete**].

Editing and controlling

There are several options for editing and controlling your WordArt object. Experiment with them as you work. Always select the object first.

To change the selected style:

1 Click the **Gallery** tool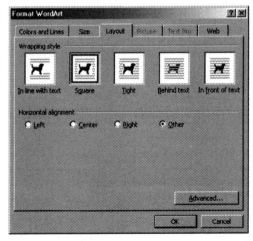

2 Choose another style and click **OK**

To edit the text in the WordArt object:

1 Click the Edit Text... tool

2 Modify the text as required and click **OK**

To change the WordArt shape:

1 Click the **Shape** tool

2 Select from the shapes displayed

To rotate the WordArt object:

◆ Drag a rotate handle (a green circle which is displayed with most Text Wrapping options) to turn the object.

To make upper and lower case characters the same height:

1 Click the **Same Letter Heights** tool

2 If it looks wrong, click again to switch the effect off

To change the way text wraps around your object:

1 Click the **Text Wrapping** tool

2 Select the wrapping option required

The **Advanced...** button gives precise control over positioning

Try out the other tools:

- Display your text vertically rather then horizontally .
- Change the alignment of your text ▥.
- Alter the spacing between your characters ⓐⓥ.

There are variations on these in the **Format WordArt** dialog box.

1   Select your WordArt object
2   Click the **Format WordArt** tool 🖼
3   Experiment with the options in the dialog box

With WordArt, a
name can
become a logo

11.2 Clip Art

If you've installed Microsoft Office you'll find you've access to
lots of Clip Art. There is also lots of Clip Art available Online
if you have access.

To insert ClipArt:

1   Click the **Insert ClipArt** tool on the
    Drawing toolbar

2   At the **Insert ClipArt** panel, enter a
    keyword, e.g. 'animal' in the **Search
    text:** field

3   Set your search options

4 Click **Search**

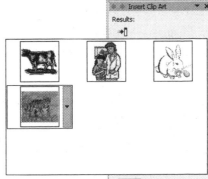

♦ If you don't enter a keyword, all available clips will be displayed.

5 Click on a picture

If you don't find anything suitable, click **Modify** at the bottom of the Task Pane and try another keyword (or leave the Search text: field empty, and scroll through all the clips to see what is available).

Clips online

If you have access to the Internet you will find hundreds of clips online.

1 Click 🌐 Clips Online in the Insert Clip Art panel

2 Read and accept the Licence agreement when it appears

3 Explore the online clips

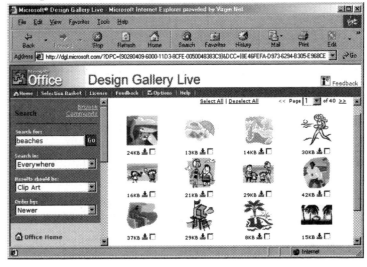

Formatting pictures

The clips can be formatted in a number of ways – experiment with the options and see what effect they have. When a clip is selected the Picture toolbar is displayed. You can use the toolbar to modify your picture.

Working from left to right on the toolbar:

◆ **Insert Picture** – uses a picture *from File* rather than from the Gallery.

◆ **Image Control** – *Automatic* is the default. *Greyscale* converts colours to shades of grey. *Black and white* converts an image to black and white. *Washout* converts it to a low contrast picture that you can place it behind everything else to create a watermark.

◆ **More Contrast** – increase the contrast.

◆ **Less Contrast** – decrease the contrast.

◆ **More Brightness** – increase the brightness.

◆ **Less Brightness** – decrease the brightness.

◆ **Crop** – lets you trim the edges of the clip.

To crop a clip:

1 Select it
2 Click the **Crop** tool
3 Drag a resizing handle to cut off the bits you don't want

◆ **Rotate Left** – rotates the image 90° to the left.

◆ **Line Style** – use to put lines around the picture, or change the line style.

◆ **Compress Pictures** – reduces the file size of the picture.

◆ **Text Wrapping** – specifies how text wraps around a picture.

◆ **Format Picture** – opens the Format Picture dialog box where you have access to even more formatting options.

◆ **Set Transparent Color** – allows you to specify one colour in a picture that will be transparent. Can be used on most pictures, except animated GIFs.

◆ **Reset Picture** – returns the clip to its original state.

11.3 Drawing Canvas

A Drawing Canvas is placed around drawing objects when you create them. You can create the Drawing Canvas, then add your objects to it, or insert the first object in your drawing and let Word automatically create the Drawing Canvas around it.

To create a Drawing Canvas:

1 Place the insertion point where you want the drawing

2 Open the **Insert** menu

3 Choose **Picture**

4 Select **New Drawing**

5 Create your drawing objects on the canvas (see 11.4)

Or

1 Select one of the drawing tools

2 Click, or click and drag to position the object

• A Drawing Canvas is placed around the object and the Drawing Canvas toolbar is displayed.

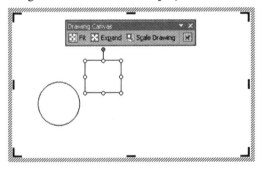

Drawing Canvas toolbar options

Fit	Resizes the Drawing Canvas to fit neatly around the objects
Expand	Makes the Drawing Canvas bigger
Scale Drawing	Resizes/scales the Drawing Canvas and the objects within it (handles appear around the Drawing Canvas that you can drag to scale).
Text Wrapping	Specifies how the text in your document wraps around your drawing

To align or distribute objects on your canvas:

1 Select the Drawing Canvas

2 Click the **Draw** tool on the Drawing Toolbar

3 Select **Align or Distribute**

4 Choose the option required

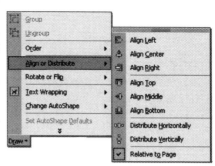

To format the Drawing Canvas:

1 Select the Drawing Canvas

2 Open the **Format** menu

3 Choose **Drawing Canvas**

11.4 Drawing tools

You can use the Drawing toolbar to add different effects to your document and also to draw your own pictures.

Line, Arrow, Rectangle and Oval

You can use these tools to draw basic lines and shapes.

To use these tools:

1 Click the tool

2 Click and drag to draw

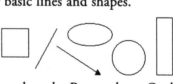

To get a perfect square or circle, select the Rectangle or Oval tool, and hold down [**Shift**] as you click and drag.

To edit or format the object, first select it then …

To resize, move or rotate your drawing objects:

* Click and drag a 'handle' to resize the object.

* Click and drag within the object to move it.

* Click and drag the rotate handle to rotate it.

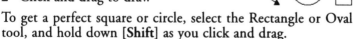

To delete a drawing object:

♦ Press [**Delete**].

To add a shadow or 3-D effect to your object:

1 Click the **Shadow** or **3-D** tool on the Drawing toolbar

2 Choose the effect you want

To change a line or arrow style of an object:

1 Click the **Line Style**, **Dash Style** or **Arrow Style** tool

2 Choose the effect you want

To change the fill colour or line colour of an object:

1 Click the drop-down arrow to the right of the **Fill** or **Line Color** tool

2 Choose a colour

Text Boxes

You can add text anywhere if it is contained within a Text Box.

To insert a Text Box:

1 Click the **Text Box** tool

2 Click and drag within the Drawing Canvas to create a Text Box

3 Type in the text you want to appear in the Text Box

4 De-select the object

When a Text Box is selected, the Text Box toolbar is displayed. You can use this to link boxes so that the overspill from one flows into the next one. You can also use it to change the alignment of text within them.

To link Text Boxes:

1 Create a Text Box and enter your text into it

2 Create another Text Box, but leave it empty

3 Select the first Text Box

4 Click the **Create Text Box Link** tool on the Text Box toolbar

5 Click on the empty Text Box that you want to link to

> The text in this Text Box

> *flows to the Text Box it is linked to*

As you enter and edit text in the first Text Box, it will flow automatically to the linked Text Box when the first box is full.

The other tools are used to break the link between Text Boxes, to move between linked Text Boxes and to change text direction.

AutoShapes

If you want to draw stars, banners, block arrows, flow chart symbols, etc. you may find the shape you need in the AutoShapes. These are just as easy to use as the basic shapes.

1 Click the **AutoShapes** tool [AutoShapes ▾] on the Drawing toolbar

2 Choose a category

3 Select a shape

4 Click and drag to draw your shape

♦ You'll find even more AutoShapes in the Clip Gallery. Choose **More Autoshapes…** from the AutoShapes categories and explore the **More AutoShapes** dialog box.

♦ The Callouts are a variation on Text Boxes – see above.

AutoShapes in action!

11.5 Draw options

The **Draw** tool on the Drawing toolbar gives access to more options. Some of them are introduced here.

♦ To open the **Draw** menu, click on the drop-down arrow to the right of the **Draw** tool on the Drawing toolbar.

Group
Ungroup
Regroup
Order ▸
Grid…
Nudge ▸
Align or Distribute ▸
Rotate or Flip ▸
Text Wrapping ▸
Reroute Connectors
Edit Points
Change AutoShape ▸
Set AutoShape Defaults

Draw ▾

Grouping

If you draw a picture using several objects, you will find your final picture easier to resize and move if you group the objects.

Before you can group objects, you must select them.

To select more than one object at a time:

1 Select the first object required

2 Hold the [**Shift**] key down while you click on each of the other objects

Or

1 Click the **Select Objects** tool on the Drawing toolbar

2 Click and drag over the objects you want to select

To group objects:

1 Select the objects you want to group

2 Click the drop-down arrow to the right of **Draw** on the Drawing toolbar

3 Choose **Group**

The objects are grouped together into one object and can then be resized, moved or deleted as one.

If you need to work on an individual object that has been grouped, you can ungroup the object again.

To ungroup an object:

1 Select the object you want to ungroup

2 Open the **Draw** menu

3 Choose **Ungroup**

Objects that have been ungrouped, can quickly be regrouped again:

1 Open the **Draw** menu

2 Choose **Regroup**

Order

When you draw your objects on top of each other, the first one you draw is on the lowest layer, the second one is on a layer above the first one, the third one on the next layer and so on.

If you end up with your objects on the wrong layer relative to each other, you can move them backwards and forwards through the layers as necessary.

To move an object from one layer to another, relative to other objects:

1 Select the object

2 Choose **Order** from the **Draw** menu

3 Move the object as required

• **Bring to Front** and **Send to Back** move the object to the top or bottom layer respectively.

• **Bring Forward** and **Send Backward** move the object one layer at a time.

• **Bring in Front of Text** and **Send Behind Text** places the object in front of or behind text in your document. The default is that a object is placed in front of text.

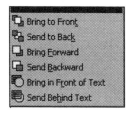

Rotate or Flip

Objects can also be rotated by any amount, or flipped 180° horizontally or vertically.

To rotate an object:

1 Select the object

2 Click the **Free Rotate** tool on the Drawing toolbar

3 Click and drag the rotate handles (small green circles) until the object is in the position required

4 Select another tool, or click the **Free Rotate** tool again, when you've finished

To flip an object:

1 Select the object

2 Choose **Rotate or Flip** from the Draw menu

3 Select a rotate or flip option

11.6 Picture fonts

You can also use any picture fonts that you have installed on your system to give you pictures.

To access the picture fonts:

1 Open the **Insert** menu and choose **Symbol**
2 Explore the fonts until you find a picture you want to use

3 Select the picture
4 Click **Insert**
5 Close the **Symbol** dialog box

You can format the character you have inserted using the Formatting toolbar or the Font dialog box – you can make it bold or put it into italics, change its size or colour, etc.

Explore the fonts that you have available to you to see if they contain any pictures that you would find useful.

Summary

In this chapter we have discussed some of the options available when you want to include special effects and pictures in a document. The main options are:

- ◆ WordArt.
- ◆ Clip Art.
- ◆ Drawing.
- ◆ Picture fonts.

12 macros

In this chapter you will learn

- about macros
- how to create, edit, run and delete macros
- how to assign new macros to tools and keyboard shortcuts

Aims of this chapter

We have already discussed some of the features that help you automate the way you work in Word. In this chapter we will consider how macros can be used to automate a routine that you perform regularly. We will discuss some areas in which you may find macros useful. You will learn how to record, play back and edit the macros you create.

12.1 What are macros?

A macro is a set of Word commands grouped together so that you can execute them as a single command. If you perform a task often, but cannot find a keyboard shortcut or tool, that runs through the sequence you want to use, you should *record* the commands into a macro. You have then created a 'custom' command.

What could you use a macro for?

◆ Speeding up routine editing and formatting.

◆ Recording the instructions to create a new document from one of your templates – your letterhead, memo or fax.

◆ Fast access to an option you regularly use in a dialog box.

◆ Combining a group of commands you often execute in the same sequence.

Two ways to create macros in Word

Recording. We will be using this option. You can record any function that you can access through the menus and dialog boxes.

Visual Basic Editor. With this you can create powerful, flexible macros that can include Visual Basic as well as Word commands. We will take a brief excursion into the Editor when we discuss editing macros.

12.2 Recording a macro

Before you start recording your macro, think through what it is that you want to record. If there are any commands that you're not sure about, try them out first to check that they do what you want to record.

For example, a macro to print the current page should record the steps:

1 Choose **Print** from the **File** menu

2 Select **Current page** in the **Page Range** options

3 Click **OK**

Once you know what you need to record, you can create your macro. In the example below we will assign the macro to a tool on a toolbar and also assign it a keyboard shortcut.

To start recording a macro:

1 Open the **Tools** menu and choose **Macro**

2 Select **Record New Macro...**

3 Enter a name (no spaces) for your macro in the **Macro name** field (don't use the default *Macro1*, *Macro2*, etc. – you'll never remember what you record in each one)

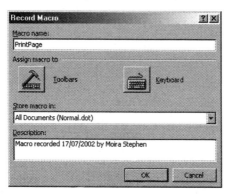

At this stage you can assign the macro to a tool on a toolbar and/or give the macro a keyboard shortcut – both are optional.

To assign a macro to a toolbar:

1 Click **Toolbars** in the **Record Macro** dialog box

• The **Customize** dialog box appears.

2 Drag the macro name from the **Commands:** list and drop it onto a toolbar that is currently displayed on screen

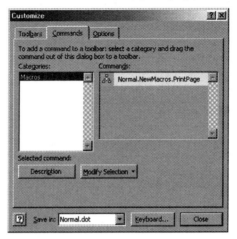

To change the button image:

1 With the tool on the toolbar still selected, click **Modify Selection** in the **Customize** dialog box

2 To display the button only on the toolbar, choose the Default style (if you opt to display text on a toolbar, each tool takes up a lot of space)

3 Click **Modify Selection** again

4 Select **Change Button Image**

5 Choose a button for your toolbar

6 Click **Close** (or **Keyboard...** if you wish to give the macro a keyboard shortcut as well)

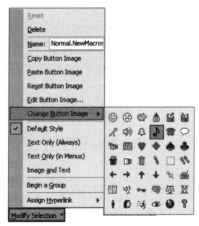

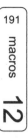
To assign a keyboard shortcut to your macro:

1 Click **Keyboard...** at the Record Macro or Customize dialog box

2 Enter a keyboard shortcut in the **Press new shortcut key:** field (you'll be told if the shortcut is already in use)

3 Click **Assign** and close the **Customize Keyboard** dialog box

4 Close the **Customize** dialog box if necessary

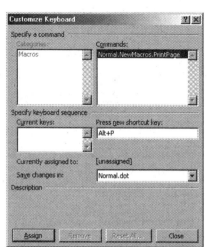

You will then be returned to your document, with the Stop Recording toolbar on display.

To record your macro:

1 Perform the sequence of commands you want to record – if you are recording the steps to print the current page, click **OK** at the **Print** dialog box to send the page to the printer

♦ If you need to temporarily stop recording your macro (perhaps to check something out) click the **Pause Recording** tool ▐◗. The tool then becomes the **Resume Recorder** tool – click it when you're ready to start recording again.

2 Click the **Stop Recording** tool ▇ when you've finished

12.3 Playing back your macro

If you assigned your macro to a toolbar:

♦ Click the tool on the toolbar to run the macro.

If you gave your macro a keyboard shortcut

♦ Press the keyboard shortcut keys to run the macro.

An alternative to running the macro from the keyboard or toolbar is to replay it through the Tools menu.

1 Open the **Tools** menu and select **Macro**
2 Choose **Macros...**
3 Select the macro you want to replay from the list
4 Click **Run**

12.4 Ideas for more macros

You can record almost anything you want into a macro. Some of the things that you could record into a macro may also be automated in other ways, e.g. AutoText or Styles. Macros are usually used to carry out a sequence of commands, or to perform tasks you would normally need to dig into a dialog box to find.

New document macros

Try out the three macros below to create three new documents. They are all easy to set up, one using your letter template, one using your memo template and one using your fax template (you could call the macros *Letter*, *Memo* and *Fax* respectively)

You would need to record these steps for each one:

1 Open the **File** menu
2 Choose **New**
3 Select **General Templates** from the Task Pane
4 Select the template you want to base your document on
5 Click **OK**

Print, Close and Create a new document

Record a macro to send the current document to print, close it and create a new blank document (you could call the macro *PrintCloseNew*)

You would need to record the steps:

1 Print the file
2 Close the file
3 Create a new blank document

Formatting macro

If you regularly apply the same formatting to a table row, record the formatting in a macro. (You could call the macro *FormatRow.*) Place the insertion point at the beginning of a row before you start to record. For example, to format a row to have shading of 30%, font Arial, size 16, colour red, with the cell contents centred you would need to record:

1 Select the entire row, by pressing [**Shift**]-[**Alt**]-[**End**] (you must use keyboard shortcuts to select when recording)

2 Open the **Format** menu and choose **Borders and Shading**

3 Select the **Shading** tab and set the shading to 30%

4 Use the formatting dialog boxes to set the font and paragraph formatting

12.5 Deleting a macro

As you experiment with setting up macros, you will inevitably end up with some that you don't want to keep. They may not prove as useful as you first thought, or they might not run properly.

To delete a macro that you no longer require:

1 Open the **Tools** menu and select **Macro**

2 Choose **Macros...**

3 Select the macro you want to delete from the list displayed

4 Click **Delete** and confirm the deletion at the prompt

5 Click **Close**

If necessary, remove the tool that executed the macro from the toolbar it was on – see section 13.3.

12.6 Editing a macro

I'd suggest you re-record any short macro that has an error in it rather than try to edit it – it's probably simpler! If you have a longer macro or have a minor adjustment to make to a macro, it's often quicker to edit it rather than re-record the whole thing.

Recorded macros are translated into Visual Basic – so things may look a bit strange when you first try editing a macro. But don't worry, if you take your time and have a look through the instructions you'll soon be able to relate your actions in Word to the Visual Basic code.

When editing a macro, be very careful not to delete anything you don't understand, or insert anything that should not be there – you might find your macro no longer runs properly if you do. If the worst comes to the worst and the macro stops working, you can always record it again.

In this example, I'm going to edit the *FormatRow* macro (see section 12.4 above) to have a font size of 18 rather than 16.

To edit the macro:

1   Open the **Tools** menu and select **Macro**

2   Choose **Macros...**

3   Select the macro you want to edit from the list and click **Edit**

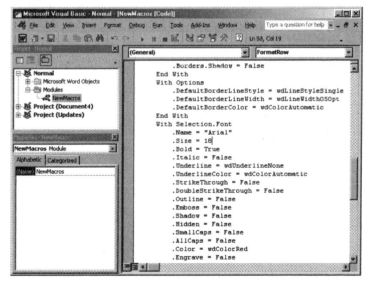

4   Scroll through the code until you see the line you want to edit

5   Edit as required – I changed the font size by deleting the **16** and typing in **18** at '**.Size =** '

6 Click the **Save Normal** tool on the toolbar

7 Close the Visual Basic Editor – click the **Close** button or choose **Close and Return to Microsoft Word** from the **File** menu

When you look through the Visual Basic code there are often far more lines of code than commands you intentionally recorded. Don't worry about this – some instructions are picked up from default settings in dialog boxes. Just scroll through until you see something you recognize as the line you want to change.

Summary

In this chapter we have discussed macros. You have learnt how to:

- Record a macro.

- Assign the macro to a toolbar.

- Give the macro a keyboard shortcut.

- Run the macro.

- Delete a macro.

- Edit a macro using the Visual Basic Editor.

toolbars

13

In this chapter you will learn

- some tricks for working with toolbars
- how to add, remove and move tools on toolbars
- how to create a new toolbar
- how to assign macros to tools

Aims of this chapter

In this chapter we discuss toolbars. We'll look at basic toolbar manipulation – showing, hiding, and positioning on the screen. We'll also discuss how you can edit existing toolbars, create new toolbars and assign to them macros that you didn't assign when you set the macro up.

13.1 Showing and hiding toolbars

You may have noticed that some toolbars appear and disappear as you work. The Picture toolbar appears when a Clip Art object is selected, the WordArt toolbar appears when a WordArt object is selected.

You can opt to show or hide toolbars whenever you want to use the tools on them. Provided you have at least one toolbar displayed, you can use the shortcut method to show or hide any toolbar.

To use the shortcut method:

1 Right-click on a toolbar

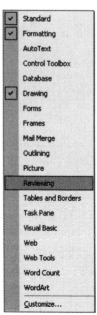

♦ Any toolbars that are displayed have a tick beside their name, any that are not displayed have no tick.

2 Click (the *left* button) on the toolbar name you wish to show or hide

If no toolbars are displayed, use the View menu to show them again.

1 Open the **View** menu and choose **Toolbars**

2 Click on the one you want to show

Using either of the methods above, you can show or hide one toolbar at a time. If you want to change the display status of several toolbars at the one time, it may be quicker to use the Customize dialog box.

1 Right-click on a toolbar or open the **View** menu and choose **Toolbars**

2 Click **Customize...**

3 On the Toolbars tab, select or deselect the toolbars in the list as required

4 Click **Close**

13.2 Moving toolbars

Toolbars can be positioned *anywhere* on your screen. There are four *docking* areas – at the top, bottom, left and right of your screen, and your toolbars can be placed in any of them. You can also leave your toolbar floating in the document area if you prefer.

The Standard and Formatting toolbars are normally displayed along the top of your screen, docked side by side, sharing one row.

To move a toolbar:

1 If the toolbar is docked, point to its left edge (if it is at the top or bottom of the screen) or top edge (if it is at the left or right of the screen) – where the darker shading is.

Or

• If it is not docked, point to its Title bar.

2 Drag and drop the toolbar to the position you want it in.

If you don't want the Standard and Formatting toolbar to share a row, you can switch this off. They can then be positioned as they were in previous versions of Word – the Standard above the Formatting toolbar.

To toggle the row-sharing option for Standard and Formatting toolbars:

1 Click the drop-down arrow at the right of the Standard or Formatting toolbar

2 Choose **Show Buttons in One Row** or **Show Buttons in Two Rows** as required

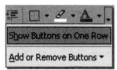

Or

1 Right-click a toolbar or choose **View, Toolbars**

2 Click on **Customize…**

3 Select the **Options** tab

4 Select or deselect the **Show Standard and Formatting toolbars on two rows** checkbox

5 Click **Close**

13.3 Editing existing toolbars

When you first start to use Word, the toolbars display several tools that perform the most regularly used Word functions, e.g. New document, Open, Save, Print. As you work, the toolbars are customized automatically to display the tools that you have used most recently.

Automatic customization of toolbars:

1 Click the drop-down arrow at the right of a toolbar

2 Select the tool required from the drop-down panel

• The tool will be placed on the main toolbar so that you can access it again quickly.

If you find that there are some tools on a toolbar that you tend not to use, or you want to add another tool to a toolbar, you can easily add or remove tools. If you want to add several tools to a toolbar, you should create a new toolbar and add your tools to it – see section 13.4. If you want to edit a toolbar it must be displayed.

Adding and removing tools:

1 Click the drop-down arrow to the right of the toolbar

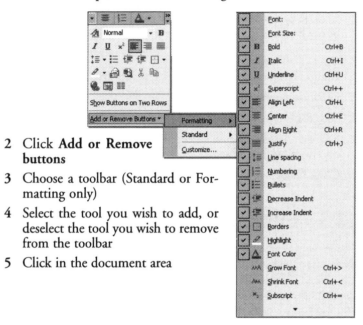

2 Click **Add or Remove buttons**

3 Choose a toolbar (Standard or Formatting only)

4 Select the tool you wish to add, or deselect the tool you wish to remove from the toolbar

5 Click in the document area

Edit an existing toolbar from the Customize dialog box:

1 Display the toolbar if necessary

2 Right-click on a toolbar or choose **View, Toolbars** or display an **Add or Remove Buttons** list

3 Click **Customize…**

4 Select the **Commands** tab

To add a tool:

1 Select the Category of tool you're looking for

2 Locate the command you require from the **Commands**: list

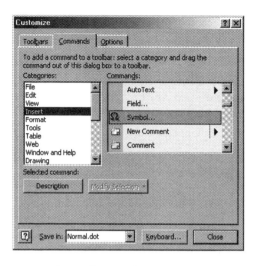

3 Drag it over to the toolbar – when you are over a toolbar a very dark I-beam with a + beside it indicates your position – and drop it in the position required (if you are not over a toolbar, the pointer has a small button with an x)

If you want a brief description of a tool's purpose, select it in the list of commands or on the toolbar, then click the **Description** button.

To move a tool:

1 Drag the tool to the correct position on the toolbar

2 Drop it

To remove a tool:

1 Drag the tool off the toolbar

2 Drop it anywhere

3 Click **Close** when you've finished editing your toolbar.

Drop-down lists on toolbars, e.g. the Style box on the Formatting toolbar, take up a lot more room than one of the picture tools. If you need to make a bit more space on a toolbar that contains drop-down tools, you can change their size as required.

To change the size of a drop-down tool, you must have the Customize dialog box open.

1 Select the tool you want to resize, e.g. Times New Roman

2   Click and drag the right or left edge of it – the mouse pointer becomes a thick double-headed arrow when you are on an edge

Shortcut

You can quickly move or delete tools from a toolbar that is displayed *without* opening the Customize dialog box.

To move a tool:

•   Hold down the [**Alt**] key and drag the tool along the toolbar (or to another toolbar).

To delete a tool:

•   Hold down the [**Alt**] key and drag the tool off the toolbar.

13.4 Creating a new toolbar

If you have several tools that you'd like to add to a toolbar (or macros that you want to assign to tools), you may find that you need to create a new toolbar, rather than try to squeeze tools into the existing toolbars.

To create a new toolbar:

1   Open the Customize dialog box

2   Select the **Toolbars** tab

3   Click **New…**

4   Give your toolbar a name and click **OK** – your toolbar will be displayed

5   Choose the **Commands** tab and add the tools you require to your new toolbar

6   Close the Customize dialog box

13.5 Adding macros to toolbars

In Chapter 12 we discussed macros – custom commands that you can set up. When setting up your macro, you have the option to assign the macro to a tool on a toolbar. However, if you opt not to add the macro to a toolbar when you create the macro, you can easily assign your macro to a tool at any time.

To assign a macro to a toolbar:

1 Display the toolbar you want to assign your macro to

2 Right-click on a toolbar or choose **View, Toolbars**

3 Click **Customize...**

4 Choose the **Commands** tab

5 Select the **Macros** category

6 Drag the macro that you want to assign to a tool over to your toolbar

• Use the Modify Selection toolbutton to edit the tool image as required (see 12.2).

7 Close the **Customize** dialog box

Summary

In this chapter we have discussed the various options available when working with and modifying toolbars. We have discussed:

• Showing and hiding toolbars.

• Positioning toolbars on your screen.

• Adding tools to toolbars.

• Removing tools from toolbars.

• Moving tools on toolbars.

• Creating new toolbars.

• Assigning macros to a tool on a toolbar.

word with other applications

In this chapter you will learn

- about linking and embedding
- how to use Word with Excel
- how to convert files between Word and PowerPoint
- about using Access data in a mail merge

Aims of this chapter

Word is part of Microsoft Office, and it integrates very well
with the other applications in the suite. If you have installed
the complete suite then you have the benefit of being able
to use the best tool for the job. This chapter discusses some
ways in which the Office applications can be integrated.

14.1 Linking vs embedding

When you work through this chapter, you will come across the
terms 'linking' and 'embedding'. Both these techniques enable
you to incorporate data from other applications into your Word
document. The main difference between linked data and embedded data lies in where it is stored and how it is updated.

Linked data

Linked data is not stored in your Word document. It is stored
in the file, e.g. a workbook or presentation, that was created
by the source application. When the data is updated within
the source application the changes are reflected in the Word
document to which it is linked.

Features of linking data include:

◆ The Word document is kept smaller.

◆ The data in the Word document is up to date.

Embedded data

Embedded data is stored in your Word document. However,
when you create and edit the data, you have access to all the
functions within the source application.

Features of embedding data:

◆ All the data is held in one document.

◆ You have access to powerful functions that are not part of
  the Word application when creating and editing the object.

The following sections discuss some of the methods you can
use to integrate data across the applications in Office.

14.2 Copy and Paste

You can copy text, data, graphics, charts, etc. from one application to another within the Office suite using simple copy and paste techniques.

To copy and paste:

1 Launch Word and the application you want to copy from
2 Select the object, text or data you want to copy
3 Click the **Copy** tool on the Standard toolbar
4 Switch to Word
5 Place the insertion point where you want the object, text or data to appear
6 Click the **Paste** tool on the Standard toolbar

Data pasted in to a Word document from Excel or Access is displayed in a Word table, and can be edited and manipulated using the table-handling features in Word.

14.3 Working with Excel data

If the data you require already exists in an Excel spreadsheet, you could copy and paste it in to your Word document (see section 14.2), or copy the data in with a *link* to the original data, or embed the data in your document.

Linking data

You can copy data into Word with a *link* to the original data in Excel. A representation of the data is displayed in Word, but the actual data is held and updated in Excel. This option is useful when file size is a consideration, or when it is important that the data in Word is kept in line with the data in Excel.

If you wish to link the data that you paste from Excel to the source file, follow the Copy and Paste instructions in 14.2, then click the **Paste Options** button and choose the link option required.

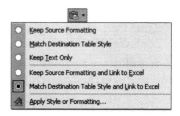

Keep Source Formatting
Match Destination Table Style
Keep Text Only
Keep Source Formatting and Link to Excel
Match Destination Table Style and Link to Excel
Apply Style or Formatting...

Linked objects

By default, linked objects are set for automatic updating. This means that the file in Word is updated automatically each time you open it, or each time the source data in Excel is updated when the destination file in Word is open. You can change the updating options in Word if you prefer. See *Control how linked objects are updated* in the *Sharing Information with other Users and Programs\Linking objects and Embedding objects folder* in the online Help for details of the options.

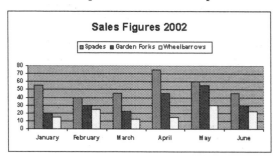

Sales Figures 2002

Gerry's Garden Centre						
2002 Purchase Record						
	January	February	March	April	May	June
Spades	25	40	45	75	60	45
Garden Forks	20	30	22	45	55	30
Wheelbarrows	15	25	12	15	30	22
TOTAL	60	95	79	135	145	97

With Paste Special, a chart copied into Word is updated if the data in the source Excel workbook is changed

Embedded data

When you embed existing data, a copy of the data is held in the Word document. You can embed the data with or without a link to the original data.

To embed existing Excel data into your Word document use Copy and Paste Special.

Embed data or a chart in Word:

1 Open the workbook that contains the data or chart
2 Select the data or chart and click the **Copy** tool
3 Switch to the Word document you want to paste into

4 Place the insertion point where you want the object to go

5 Open the **Edit** menu and choose **Paste Special...**

6 Select the **Paste Link** button if you want a link to the original data

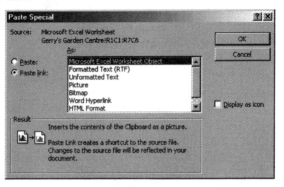

7 Choose **As Excel Worksheet Object** from the **As:** list

8 Click **OK**

If you embed an object with the Paste link: option selected, the data in Word is updated each time you update the data in Excel. If you double-click on the object in Word, the Excel file is opened so that you can update it and save. The changes are reflected in the Word document.

If you choose the Paste: option, you can edit the data in Word by double-clicking on the object. All the Excel tools and menus are displayed so that you can work on the embedded data, but the changes are not reflected in the original Excel file.

Insert an Excel worksheet

If you want an Excel worksheet in your Word document, but don't need the worksheet for any other purpose, you can insert one into your document. The worksheet will be created and edited using Excel functions. An Excel worksheet inserted in this way is an 'embedded' object.

To insert an Excel worksheet:

1 Place the insertion point where you want the worksheet to go

2 Click the **Insert Microsoft Excel Worksheet** tool

3   Click and drag over the grid to specify the worksheet size

◆   This creates an embedded worksheet, with the toolbars and menus of Excel displayed.

4   Set up the worksheet using Excel's tools and menus

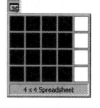

5   Click anywhere outside the worksheet area when you've finished

◆   To return to Excel to edit the worksheet, double-click on it.

14.4 Word and PowerPoint

To create a link to a slide in PowerPoint:

1   Open the presentation that contains the slide

2   Go into **Slide Sorter** view and select the slide required

3   Click the **Copy** tool

4   Switch to the Word document you want to paste into

5   Place the insertion point where you want the slide to go

6   Open the **Edit** menu and choose **Paste Special…**

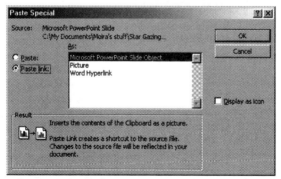

7   Select the **Paste Link** button

8   Choose an option from the **As:** list

9   Click **OK**

If the PowerPoint presentation is updated, you must save the changes before they will be reflected in your Word document.

PowerPoint presentation from Word documents

As well as copy and paste, there are other ways to work between PowerPoint and Word.

You can set up a PowerPoint presentation from a Word document. The document must be set up as an outline (see section 8.7), and formatted using the heading styles 1–9 as PowerPoint uses these to structure the new slides. Text formatted as *Heading 1* style will be used for the slide titles, *Heading 2* styles for the first level of bullet points, etc.

To create the presentation:

1 Open your Word document if necessary
2 Choose **Send To** from the **File** menu
3 Click **Microsoft PowerPoint**

Word documents from PowerPoint presentations

You can also quickly generate a Word document from a PowerPoint presentation. The print quality of the presentation is improved if you switch to a black and white colour scheme before you send your presentation (Open the **View** menu in PowerPoint and click **Black and White**).

1 Open the presentation you want to create a document from
2 Choose **Send To** from the **File** menu
3 Select **Microsoft Word**
4 Choose a page layout in the Write-Up dialog box
5 Select **Paste** or **Paste Link**
6 Click **OK**

A new document will be created in Word. You can save and/or print the document as required.

If you Paste link, your Word document will automatically up-date when the PowerPoint presentation is edited and saved.

Meeting Minder

If you use Meeting Minder to take notes as you give a presen-tation in PowerPoint, you can export the notes and actions to Word at the end of your presentation.

1 Click **Export...** in the **Meeting Minder** dialog box

2 Select **Send meeting minutes and action items to Microsoft Word**

3 Click **Export Now**

The result is a quickly produced summary of the meeting.

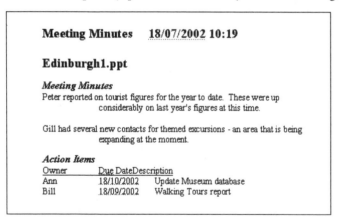

14.5 Word and Access

You can copy and paste from Access in the same way as from Excel. You can also use an Access table or query as a data source in a Mail Merge (see section 10.2).

To use an Access table or query as a data source in Mail Merge:

1 Create or open your main document

2 Click **Open Data Source** on the **Mail Merge** toolbar

3 Locate the database that you want to link to your main document

4 Open the database

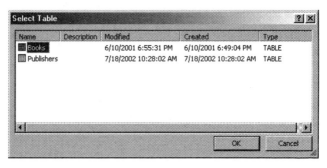

5 Select the **Table** or **Query** you want to link to

6 Click **OK**

◆ You can also link to an Excel worksheet in the same way.

◆ You can select any worksheet or named range as your data source.

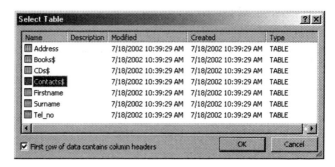

Summary

In this chapter we have discussed some of the ways you can integrate Word with the rest of the Microsoft Office suite. We have discussed:

+ Linking and embedding

+ Copy and Paste.

+ Linking and embedding existing Excel data

+ Inserting an Excel worksheet into a Word document.

+ Linking to PowerPoint slides

+ Creating a PowerPoint presentation from a Word document.

+ Creating a Word document from a PowerPoint presentation.

+ Creating minutes in Word from Meeting Minder in PowerPoint.

+ Using an Access table or query as the data source document in a Word mail merge.

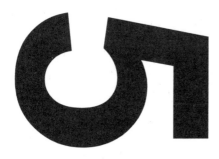

word and the web

In this chapter you will learn

- how to e-mail from Word
- about creating hyperlinks
- how to create a Web site
- about adding themes to your Web site
- how to find out how to publish your Web site

Aims of this chapter

This chapter discusses using Word with the wider world.
You will learn how to e-mail a document (you must have e-mail software). You will also learn how to use hyperlinks to link to other files on your own computer or network, and to pages on the World Wide Web. Finally, we'll create a Web document in Word and discuss how to publish it to the Web.
The examples are based on the use of Outlook for e-mail.
You must have access to the Internet for this chapter.

15.1 E-mail

Provided you have a modem, communications software and an Internet service provider, you can e-mail your Word documents to anywhere in the world. E-mail is usually very fast – sometimes your message will be delivered almost instantly, and it rarely takes more than an hour.

To e-mail directly from Word you must have the document you wish to send open. It can either be sent as a mail message or as an attachment.

To e-mail a document from within Word:

1 Open the document you want to e-mail

2 Click **E-mail** on the Standard toolbar

Or

♦ Choose **Send To** from the **File** menu.

3 Select **Mail Recipient...** to send the document as the content of your message

Or

♦ Select **Mail Recipient (as Attachment)** to send the document as an attachment to your message.

4 Enter the e-mail address you want to send the message to (or select it from your Address Book – see below)

5 Enter or edit the subject as necessary

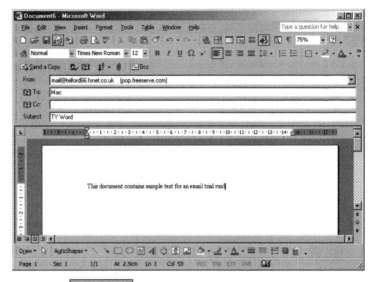

6 Click Send a Copy (if you chose **Mail Recipient** at 3 above) or (if you are sending it as an attachment)

7 Close your message

A record of the items you send is kept in the **Sent Items** folder in Outlook.

• If you've never used e-mail before, take time to have a look at the package you have installed to find out what it can do.

To read any documents you may be sent, you must open your e-mail application and locate the message in your inbox.

Address Book

The Address Book is part of Outlook. You can store details of your contacts in the Address Book, and access their details when required. You can access the Address Book from Outlook, or from Word, when sending an e-mail.

To enter an e-mail address from the Address Book:

1 Click the Address Book icon to the left of **To:** or **Cc:**

2 Select the recipient from the list down the left of the **Select Recipients** dialog box

3 Click the **To: Cc:** or **Bcc:** buttons (down the middle of the dialog box) to put the address into the correct field

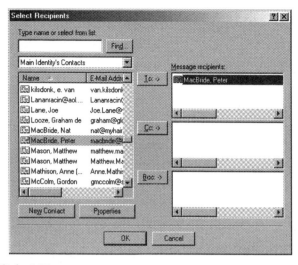

4 Click **OK**

◆ To delete an address from the **To: Cc:** or **Bcc:** fields, select it and press the [**Delete**] key.

◆ To add a person to the Address Book, click the **New Contact** button, enter the details into the tabs and click **OK**.

◆ To check or edit the details held on any contact, select the contact name from the list and click **Properties**. Amend the details as necessary and click **OK**.

15.2 Hyperlinks

A hyperlink is a 'hot spot' that lets you jump from your document to another location – on your own computer, on your company network or anywhere in the world via the Internet.

You can insert a hyperlink anywhere in your document. When you click a hyperlink, the file that it points to is displayed on your screen.

To insert a hyperlink to a file:

1 Click the **Insert Hyperlink** tool ![icon] on the Standard toolbar

2 Select **Existing File or Web Page** in the **Link to:** options

3 Enter the text you wish displayed in your document

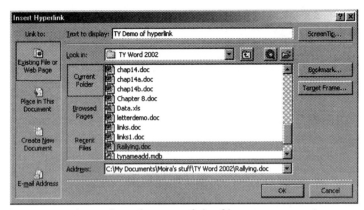

4 Type in the path and name of the file you want to jump to

Or

• Locate the file on your system using the list of folders and files.

5 If you wish to jump to a bookmark in the selected file, click **Bookmark…** and select the one from the dialog box

6 Click **OK** at the **Insert Hyperlink** dialog box

The hyperlink will be inserted into your document. The text usually appears blue, with an underline. In the example, the hyperlinked text is '<u>TY Demo of hyperlink</u>', and it opens the file *C:\My Document\Moira's Stuff\TYWord 2002\ Rallying.doc.*

To insert a hyperlink to a URL on the Web:

1 Click the **Insert Hyperlink** tool

2 Select **Existing File or Web Page** in the **Link to:** options

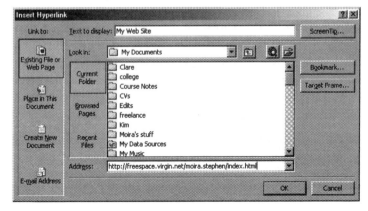

3 Enter the text you wish to display in your document

4 Type in the URL (Uniform Resource Locator, the Internet address) of the page you want to jump to

5 Click **OK** at the **Insert Hyperlink** dialog box – your hyperlink text will be displayed, e.g. <u>My Web Site</u>

To insert a hyperlink to an area in the current document:

1 Click the **Insert Hyperlink** tool

2 Select **Place in This Document** in the **Link to:** options

3 Select the **Top of Document**, **Headings** or **Bookmarks**

4 Choose the Heading or Bookmark if necessary

5 Click **OK**

To jump to a hyperlink location:

♦ Hold down [**Ctrl**] and click on the hyperlink

When you jump to a hyperlink location, the Web toolbar is displayed.

To return to the position in the document you jumped from, click the **Back** tool on the Web toolbar.

Once you've jumped to a hyperlink, then returned to your document, the hyperlink field changes colour – usually to violet. This will remind you that you've already used that hyperlink.

To edit a hyperlink:

1 Right-click on the hyperlink

2 Select **Edit Hyperlink...**

3 Edit the display text and address as necessary

4 Click **OK**

To remove a hyperlink, but leave the text displayed:

1 Right-click on the hyperlink in your document

2 Select **Remove Hyperlink**

To delete the hyperlink and the text:

♦ Select the hyperlink and press [**Delete**].

15.3 Preparing a Web page

In this electronic age, a lot of information is distributed electronically, using e-mail and the Internet. If you feel that you can reach your target audience over the Internet, you could use Word to help you create a Web page or a whole Web site.

Before you start to set up your Web site, spend some time looking at other people's sites. Find out what you like and don't like about the way some of the pages are presented.

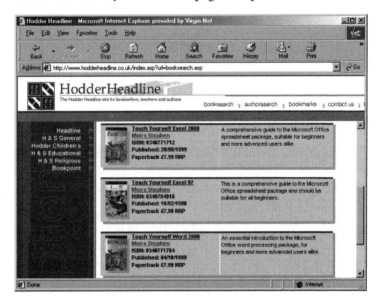

Don't try to put everything you want to say on one page. Use the first page (the home page) of the site to give your visitor an overview of it and to point them to other information that they may be interested in.

You may notice that some Web pages fill the whole screen. On others, the information is displayed in separate frames on the page – where you can scroll the information in each frame independently from the other frames. You can create Web pages with or without frames in Word – but remember that not all Web browsers can support frames, so your may find that pages with frames do not display properly in some browsers.

15.4 Creating a Web site

The easiest way to create a Web site is to use the Web Page Wizard.

1 Open the **File** menu and choose **New**
2 Select **General Templates** on the New Document task pane
3 Select the **Web Pages** tab
4 Choose **Web Page Wizard**
5 Click **OK**

The Web Page Wizard will help you set up your Web site. Simply give the information requested at each step in the wizard and click **Next**.

Step 1

Give your Web site a **title** and select the folder in which you store the Web site files. When you publish your site (see section 15.6) you will need to copy this folder to your Internet service provider's computer.

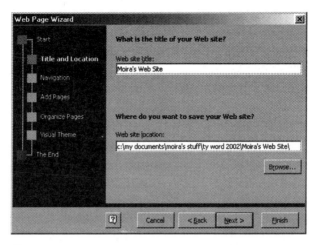

Step 2

Do you want a vertical or horizontal frame for navigation, or do you want to use separate pages? Select one and click **Next**.

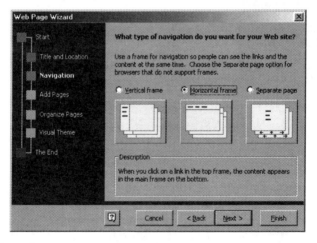

Step 3

To add more pages

1   Click **Add Template Page...**

2   Select the page you want

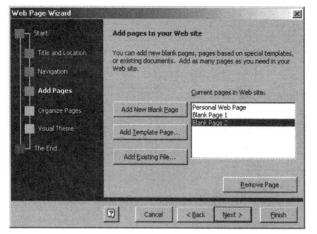

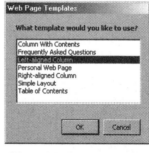

3 Click **OK**

4 Repeat 1–3 until you've added the pages that you need

♦ To remove any page, select it and click **Remove Page**.

Step 4

You can change the order of the pages. To reorganize your pages:

1 Select the page you wish to move

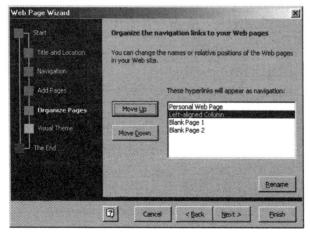

2   Click **Move Up** or **Move Down** until it is in the right place

You should rename pages so that their titles describe their contents. If your don't rename them, they'll be called *Blank Page 1*, etc.

1   Select the page

2   Click **Rename**

3   Enter the new name

4   Click **OK**

Step 5

You can give your site a professional finish by using a theme.

1   Select **Add a visual theme**

2   Click **Browse Themes...**

3 Choose the theme you wish to use

4 Click **OK**

Click **Finish** at the final step in the wizard, and sit back while Word does all the work!

15.5 Customizing your site

The wizard will set up a site using the information that you provided as you worked through the steps. Hyperlinks will have been inserted so that you can jump around the site. Explore your site to see how it works.

Word will have inserted instructions throughout the Web site telling you what to do e.g. 'type some text' or 'insert a hyperlink' (see section 15.2). Follow the prompts on the screen to personalize your site.

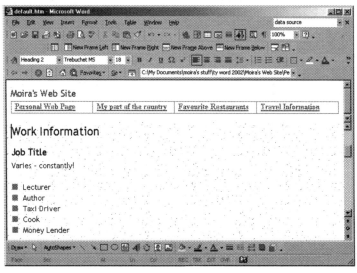

- If you wish to change the theme, open the **Format** menu, choose **Theme...**, pick a one from the list and click **OK**.

- If you wish to change any Clip Art, select and delete the existing picture, and choose another one from the Gallery.

- Click the **Save** tool on the Standard toolbar to save your Web site and close it.

• If you want to open your site again to edit it in Word, open the **default** file in the folder that you saved your Web site in at Step 1.

15.6 Publishing to the Web

To publish your HTML file to the Web you must transfer your file from your own computer to a server that is provided by your service provider (unless you want your own computer to become a server on the Web). Your service provider's server will be switched on 24 hours a day so anyone who knows the URL of your Web page will be able to access it at any time.

Most service providers will allocate some free space to you for your own Web pages – 10 Mb (about 7 diskettes worth) is fairly typical. There are a number of ways to upload files to a service provider's server – contact your service provider to find out how to upload your files to their server.

If you have created hyperlinks in your Web page or site that jump to other files on your computer, remember to upload *all* the files needed, not just the main page.

Summary

This final chapter has discussed ways in which you can interact with the wider world from Word. We have discussed how you can:

• Send e-mail messages from Word.

• Create hyperlinks to other files, Web pages and bookmarks.

• Create a Web page or Web site.

• Add a theme to your Web pages.

• Find out how to publish your Web pages.

taking it further

If you've mastered half of what's in this book, you are well on the way to becoming a proficient Word user. If you are getting to grips with most of it, you are doing very well indeed.

You'll find lots of information on Word on the Internet, in addition to the Help menu option **Office on the Web** that takes you to the site:

http://office.microsoft.com/uk/assistance/

Other sites that you may find useful include:

http://www.microsoft.com/office/word/default.asp

http://search.support.microsoft.com/search/

You could also try searching the Web for sites that provide information on Word. Try entering "Microsoft Word" + "Software Reviews" into your search engine. You should come up with several sites worth a look.

If you would like to join a course to consolidate your skills, you could try your local college, or search the Internet for on-line courses. Most courses cost money, but you may find the odd free one – try those at:

http://www.baycongroup.com/wlesson0.htm

Good Word skills are useful on many levels – personal, educational and vocational. Now that you have improved your Word skills, why not try for certification? The challenge of an exam can be fun, and a recognized certificate may improve your job prospects. There are a number of different bodies that you could consider.

You may want to consider MOUS exams (Microsoft Office User Specialist) or ECDL (European Computer Driving Licence – basic or advanced) certification. Or, if you feel more ambitious, how about other Microsoft Certified Professional exams!

Visit:

http://www.microsoft.com/traincert/mcp/mous/

for information on MOUS certification or

http://www.ecdl.com

for information on ECDL.

index